THE CARIBBEAN

THE

CARIBBEAN

ISSUES IN U.S. RELATIONS

RAYMOND CARROLL

FRANKLIN WATTS
New York ■ London ■ Toronto ■ Sydney ■ 1984
AN IMPACT BOOK

Map courtesy of Vantage Art, Inc.

Carroll, Raymond.
The Caribbean—issues in U.S. relations.

(An Impact book)
Bibliography: p.
Includes index.
Summary: Discusses Caribbean history and politics,
emphasizing the struggle between western-style democratic
values and Marxist-Leninist doctrine and the role of the
United States in the Caribbean.
1. Caribbean Area—History—Juvenile literature.
2. Caribbean Area—Relations—United States—Juvenile
literature.   3. United States—Relations—Caribbean Area
—Juvenile literature.   [1. Caribbean Area—History.
2. Caribbean Area—Relations—United States.   3. United
States—Relations—Caribbean Area]   I. Title.   II. Title:
Caribbean—issues in US relations.
F2176.C37 1984   972.9   84-10392
ISBN 0-531-04852-7

CONTENTS

THE CARIBBEAN

INTRODUCTION

In the early years of the 1980s, the world—and the United States in particular—was compelled by events to pay greater attention to the Caribbean. The events in question were not pleasant ones: the exodus from Cuba to the United States of a new wave of refugees totaling 125,000 people; the pathetic attempt of tens of thousands of Haitian "boat people" to find new lives on the American mainland; military coups in Suriname and Grenada; and the American-led armed intervention in Grenada at the urgent request of the tiny island's closest Caribbean neighbors.

The picture, of course, was not totally unpleasant. Most of the governments of the Caribbean countries were stable and democratic, despite difficult economic and social conditions. The idyllic, sun-splashed beaches remained a magnet for tourists from around the world. But for many of the over 30 million people of the Caribbean, the carefree life of the travel brochures had little to do with reality. Many people of the area endured bitter economic and political deprivation; large numbers left the Caribbean to seek a better life somewhere else.

THE CARIBBEAN

Language
- English
- French
- Spanish
- Dutch

UNITED STATES

ATLANTIC
OCEAN

BAHAMAS

CUBA

GREATER ANTILLES

HAITI

DOMINICAN REPUBLIC

PUERTO RICO

JAMAICA

U.S. VIRGIN ISLANDS

ST. MARTIN

SABA

ST. EUSTATIUS

GUADELOUPE

LEEWARD ISLANDS

MARTINIQUE

BARBADOS

GRENADA

WINDWARD ISLANDS

LESSER ANTILLES

TRINIDAD AND TOBAGO

CARIBBEAN
SEA

CURACAO

ARUBA

BONAIRE

Panama Canal

MEXICO

BELIZE

GUATEMALA

HONDURAS

EL SALVADOR

NICARAGUA

COSTA RICA

PANAMA

PACIFIC
OCEAN

COLOMBIA

VENEZUELA

GUYANA

SURINAME

FRENCH GUIANA

Like many other parts of the world, the Caribbean is beset by political conflict. Conservatives and moderates of one coloration or another vie with reformers and radicals of various hues. Some of them believe they know the solutions to the region's problems; others simply would like to wield power. But perhaps the most potentially explosive aspect of Caribbean political life in the 1980s is the struggle between the believers in Western-style democratic values on one side and the proponents of Marxism-Leninism on the other. In simple terms, one believes that the best hope for progress is found in societies providing political liberty, economic pluralism, and close ties to the democratic world, especially the United States. The other is convinced that Caribbean societies must be radically transformed and that this can be accomplished only by all-powerful one-party states with centrally controlled economies and strong bonds with the Soviet Union and its allies. The conflict has split countries, families, and friends. It carries the seeds of major violent upheavals in the future.

Following scholarly tradition, this book considers the following as parts of the Caribbean region: (1) the many islands which are the peaks of a submerged mountain chain and which stretch from the tip of Florida to the coast of Venezuela; (2) the three Guianas (now known as French Guiana, Guyana, and Suriname; and (3) Belize (formerly British Honduras). The Guianas and Belize are coastal states on the South and Central American mainlands, but they share with the islands a common history of colonization, plantation economies, slavery, and an Afro-European cultural heritage.

A word of explanation about terms is also in order. The islands of the Caribbean, excluding the Bahamas, are sometimes referred to as the Antilles. The Greater Antilles are Cuba, Jamaica, Puerto Rico, and Hispaniola (Haiti and the Dominican Republic). The Lesser Antilles are the smaller islands. When the Caribbean Basin is mentioned, it refers to the Caribbean islands and mainland states plus Venezuela, Colombia, and Central America.

CHAPTER 1
THE CARIBBEAN TODAY

Just what is this Caribbean region we are talking about? Almost every student of the Caribbean has asked this question in one form or another. Do we treat the region simply as a motley collection of countries, each with its own particularity? Or do the nearly thirty colonies and former colonies actually add up to a single cultural area?

It is easy enough to spot the diversity that marks the Caribbean. Except for an almost uniformly pleasant climate and a location in the northern tropics to the southeast of the United States and to the north of South America, the various Caribbean countries seem to differ from each other as much as bananas do from bauxite. Physically, the countries range from fairly sizable mainland states to the tiniest of islands. The political systems are just as varied, running the gamut from parliamentary democracies to Marxist dictatorships.

The people of the Caribbean are also a striking mixture. Depending on the particular colonial experience, the major language of any given place may be English, Spanish, French, or Dutch. Outside the cities, you can hear local mixtures of European and African tongues such as the English-based Taki-Taki and the Dutch-based Papiamento, as well as a variety of Amerindian dialects. The people who speak these languages are, in order of their ancestors' appearance in the Caribbean, Amerindians, the descendants of European settlers, Afro-Americans, a variety of Asians, including Chinese, Indians, and Javanese, as well as every imaginable ethnic combination. The variety of racial strains has made Caribbeans especially conscious of skin color, and even in the 20th century it has remained an important factor in fixing a person's place in the scheme of things. Writer V. S. Naipaul recalls that during his childhood in Trinidad people were carefully classified by complexion as "white, fusty, musty, dusty, tea, coffee, cocoa, light black, black, dark black."

The enormous variation among the people and countries of the Caribbean is not open to question. But neither is the history that binds one Caribbean citizen to another. Trinidadians may look down on Grenadians, as many of them do; the people of Haiti and the Dominican Republic, neighbors on the island of Hispaniola, may despise each other, as large numbers do; but most educated inhabitants of the area recognize that there is a regional kinship that makes them all Caribbean.

The kinship stems from a common heritage: colonization by European powers and the establishment of plantation economies producing crops such as sugar and tobacco for export; the importation of African slaves and indentured Asian servants over a period of centuries; the gradual creation of mixed-race societies; the slow retreat of the European powers and the hard-won battle for independence; the dominant influence of the United States in the 20th century; the continuing struggle to diversify their agricultural societies and lessen dependence on outside powers; and the steady emigration of people in search of economic and political betterment. All these factors have played a role in creating the cultural entity we call the Caribbean.

For the sake of clarity, we can break down the countries of the Caribbean into groups.

ENGLISH-SPEAKING COUNTRIES

The hundreds of islands that once made up Britain's Caribbean empire are now grouped into seventeen political units, twelve of which had gained their independence by 1983.

Of these the four most important are Jamaica, Barbados, Trinidad and Tobago, and the mainland state of Guyana. All of these, as well as the smaller, independent English-speaking countries, adopted Britain's system of parliamentary democracy and remain members of the British Commonwealth. As head of government, these countries, like Britain, have a prime minister who reflects the political balance in parliament. With the exception of Grenada, all have maintained the democratic tradition, preserving political freedoms, opposition parties, and open, hard-fought elections.

Parliamentary tradition aside, there is considerable variation within the English-speaking group. In Jamaica and Barbados, blacks form the large majority, with whites and people of mixed race making up small minorities. The ethnic composition of Trinidad and Tobago and Guyana is more complex. Blacks are in a majority in Trinidad and Tobago and dominate politics there, but East Indians make up three-eighths of the population and are a major political force. In Guyana, the East Indians actually have a majority, although a black-dominated party has governed since independence in 1966. In both Trinidad and Tobago and Guyana, the major political parties draw most of their support from one ethnic group or another. The East Indian

■6■

community, however, is less able to act as a solid bloc, because of sectarian differences between Hindus and Muslims.

The other English-speaking entities in the Caribbean are a mixed lot. Belize, an independent country tucked into the east coast of Central America between Mexico and Guatemala, is comparatively large but thinly populated and very poor. Antigua, the Bahamas, Dominica, St. Kitts-Nevis, St. Lucia and St. Vincent-Grenadines are independent mini-states, all of which follow the British model of parliamentary democracy.

Other islands or groups of islands remain under British control. As of early 1984, these included Anguilla, Montserrat, the Cayman Islands, the Turks and Caicos Islands and the British Virgin Islands.

SPANISH-SPEAKING COUNTRIES

The two independent countries of Cuba and the Dominican Republic, along with the Commonwealth of Puerto Rico, are the remains of the once-great Spanish empire in the Caribbean.

After years of dictatorial rule followed by turmoil and U.S. intervention, the Dominican Republic has had a succession of democratically elected governments closely aligned with the United States. It is located on the eastern half of the island of Hispaniola, which it shares—not always comfortably—with the Republic of Haiti.

Cuba, the largest and most populous of the Caribbean islands, has been the region's most troublesome country in recent years. Following Marxist-Leninist political philosophy, the "Pearl of the Antilles" has a one-party state which prohibits personal and political freedoms, aligns itself closely with the Soviet Union, and tries to export its revolutionary ideas to other parts of the Caribbean and beyond.

Puerto Rico is something of an anomaly in the Caribbean. Not an independent country and not a colony, the Commonwealth of Puerto Rico is a state "freely associated" with the United States. Its people, who enjoy the highest standard of living in the Caribbean, have voted freely to retain this special status rather than become an independent country or a state in the United States. Puerto Ricans are citizens of the United States and can move freely to and from the mainland.

FRENCH AND DUTCH CARIBBEAN

Originally French colonies, French Guiana, Martinique, and Guadeloupe also have a peculiar political status. They are now "departments" of France, much as Hawaii or Alaska are states in the United States, and elect delegates to the French National Assembly in Paris. All three, however, have militant, sometimes violent, nationalist movements determined to achieve total independence.

Haiti was also a French colony, but after a bloody social revolution led by African slaves it became an independent country in 1804. It is the poorest country in the hemisphere and one of the most troubled. French-speaking, largely black, Haiti was ruled by a mulatto upper class until its overthrow in the 1950s. Since then it has endured a succession of brutal dictators who are seemingly unconcerned about the welfare of the people.

The only part of the Dutch Caribbean to have gained independence by 1984 was Suriname, a country on the South American mainland. It has one of the richest mixtures of ethnic groups—including Amerindians, Europeans, African-Americans and Asians—of any country in the region. Multi-party coalitions ruled for a while after independence in 1975, but in 1980 the government was taken over by the military. In addition to an ambitious military force, Suriname is burdened by extreme ethnic, linguistic, and religious fragmentation.

Other Dutch remnants in the Caribbean include the islands of Aruba, Bonaire, St. Eustatius, Curaçao, Saba and St. Maarten, all of which remain under the control of the Netherlands.

THE AMERICAN CARIBBEAN

St. Thomas, St. Croix and St. John make up the U.S. Virgin Islands. They were purchased from Denmark in 1917 for $25 million and are the only U.S.–owned territories in the region. In 1927, Virgin Islanders became citizens of the United States. The governor of the islands is elected locally and democratically.

CHAPTER
■2■
INDIANS
AND
EUROPEANS

The written history of the Caribbean began in 1492, with the arrival of Christopher Columbus's first expedition to the New World. But people had been living in the region for a long time before that. Archaeologists and historians now know that the first group of people to enter the Caribbean were the Ciboneys (or Siboneys), followed by the Arawaks and Caribs, for whom the area is named. When the *Niña, the Pinta,* and the *Santa Maria* sailed into Caribbean waters with the first Europeans, the Indian inhabitants numbered around 750,000, most of them on the island of Hispaniola.

BEGINNINGS

The Ciboney people were nomadic hunters and gatherers who probably migrated into the Caribbean from northern South America. They came a thousand years or more before Columbus, but very few were left by the time he arrived, since the Arawaks and then the Caribs had moved into the region and wiped out most of the more primitive

Ciboneys. Archaeological sites reveal no evidence that the Ciboneys were advanced enough to practice agriculture. They made no pottery or utensils; their only weapons were clubs or stones thrown by hand. It seems likely that the Ciboneys almost certainly were too primitive to have developed complicated religious rituals or social organization. Far more is known about the other two pre-Columbian groups of Amerindians.

The Arawaks almost certainly came from the forests between the Orinoco and Amazon rivers on the South American continent and migrated northward across the Caribbean islands, either in search of better living conditions or in flight before the warlike Caribs. The latter had been pushing into Arawak territory from an area astride the borders of modern Brazil and Bolivia.

Whatever the reason for the Arawak migration, they spread across the Antilles from the coast of Venezuela to the Bahamas in the north. They were subsistence farmers, growing maize, cassava, peanuts, peppers, and beans, chiefly for their own use but perhaps a small amount for trade. Some of the Arawaks were advanced enough to dig irrigation ditches, fertilize fields with ash or urine, and block inland rivers to form fish ponds. No large wild animals existed on the islands, but the Arawaks did eat small animals such as lizards, bats, and rabbits. A creative people, the Arawaks made decorated pottery and wove baskets; they fashioned tools of bone, stone, wood, and shell.

Columbus was quite impressed by the Arawaks he encountered on his first journey to the Caribbean. He wrote:

They were all very well built with fine bodies and handsome faces. Their hair is coarse, almost like that of a horse's tail. . . . . They are the color of the Canary Islanders, neither black nor white. . . . They have no metal. Their spears are made of cane. Some, instead of an iron tip, have fish's tooth and others have points of different kinds. . . . I believe that they would easily be made into Christians, for they appeared to me to have no religion.

Columbus was wrong about the last point. The Arawaks had a highly complex religion based on a mixture of nature worship, ancestor worship, and protective magic. They also had developed a degree of social organization and hereditary chiefs ("caciques"), who had considerable prestige in limited areas but little authority to rule. When a cacique was sick or injured and could no longer carry out his duties, he was strangled and replaced by his eldest son. But on the whole, the Arawaks were a nonviolent, even-tempered people, and Columbus wrote that "there is in my opinion no better people and no better land in all the world. . . they love their neighbors as themselves and their way of speaking is the sweetest in the world, always gentle and smiling."

The Caribs were an entirely different matter. Though they were quite similar to the Arawaks in many ways, farming and fishing, making pottery, utensils, and furniture such as simple tables and stools, they were a fierce people who worshiped an evil god named Maboya as well as many sea spirits. They, too, had hereditary chiefs, but their military leaders were elected by males of a war-making age. By the time Columbus arrived, the aggressive Caribs had followed the Arawaks into the Caribbean, had destroyed their settlements in the Lesser Antilles, and were raiding the larger islands. Their war canoes, made from the trunks of huge trees, carried more than a hundred warriors and struck terror into the hearts of the more peaceful Arawaks. What is more, the Caribs had advanced weapons: bows and arrows tipped with poison, javelins, and clubs with sharp flints fixed in their heads. After a successful raid, the Caribs carried away the Arawak women and children into slavery; the Arawak men were killed or ritualistically cooked and eaten.

The Arawaks, despite their many good qualities, could not defend themselves against the Caribs. It is likely that the Caribs would have gained the upper hand throughout the Caribbean—if the Spanish had not arrived on the scene.

ENTER COLUMBUS

In his search for the East Indies and their fabled wealth, Columbus and his three caravels crossed the Atlantic in thirty-six days and landed on a tiny island in the Bahamas which he christened San Salvador ("Holy Savior"). It was a momentous event in the history of modern man. The Vikings and Irish may have preceded Columbus to the New World, far to the north, but this was the beginning of regular contact between Europe and America—a contact that was to give new directions to the history of Europe, America, Africa, and Asia. For the Indians of the Caribbean, the coming of Columbus spelled inevitable doom.

Columbus was disappointed to find no gold, jewels, or spices on San Salvador, and so he sailed south and then east until he reached the island of Hispaniola. There his largest ship, the *Santa Maria,* ran aground and sank. The Spaniards were received hospitably by the resident Arawaks, but once again they found none of the abundant riches they expected. Reluctantly, Columbus temporarily gave up his search for the opulent Asia of his dreams and sailed for Spain in his two remaining ships. Thirty-nine men had to be left behind, and they built a fort from the timbers of the wrecked Santa Maria and called it La Navidad. These were the first European settlers in the Caribbean.

In the following year, Columbus sailed for the Caribbean again, this time with a fleet of seventeen ships and over 1,200 men. Arriving in Hispaniola in November 1493, he found that the fort built a year earlier had been destroyed and the garrison killed by the Arawaks. What had incurred the wrath of the normally pacific Indians? We are not certain. The answer can be surmised, however, from what took place when Columbus left Hispaniola briefly in 1494 to explore the southern coast of Cuba and circumnavigate Jamaica. On his return to Hispaniola he found that the Spaniards there had abandoned work on farms and the construction of buildings. Instead, they were forcing the Arawaks to provide them with food, trinkets, and women. As a result, the resentful Indians once again had taken up arms against the Spaniards.

Columbus was angered by the conduct of the Spanish settlers and punished some of them with prison terms and forced labor, but he also decided that it was necessary to crush the resistance of the Arawaks to Spanish rule. It was, of course, an unequal contest. The Indians had only the most primitive weapons. The Spaniards had steel swords, crossbows, and metal-tipped pikes. Their armor-covered horses terrified people who had never before seen an animal larger than a rabbit. In short order, tens of thousands of Arawaks were killed. The Spaniards had made it clear that they were in charge on the island of Hispaniola.

Columbus returned to Spain in 1496, but he left Spanish settlers and soldiers firmly entrenched on Hispaniola. The Arawaks were forced to pay taxes of spun cotton and whatever gold they could scrape together. Those who resisted were hunted down and massacred; others died from smallpox, a disease brought to the New World by the Spaniards. One estimate is that between 200,000 and 300,000 Arawaks lived on Hispaniola before Columbus arrived. By 1496, approximately two thirds had been killled, either by Spanish arms or disease.

Columbus was to make two more journeys to the Caribbean. On his third voyage, in 1498, he discovered Trinidad and sailed to within miles of the South American mainland; on his fourth voyage, in 1502, he explored much of the Central American coast. Though his dream of finding a route to Asia and its riches was never realized, he had achieved much for Spain. He discovered the best ocean routes to and from the Caribbean and Central America. Columbus found a new world, whose wealth would make Spain the richest and most powerful country in Europe.

COLONIZING THE CARIBBEAN

After Columbus, the monarchs of Spain sent practical administrators and thousands of settlers of every class to strengthen and expand their control. The Spanish church, eager for conversions to Christianity, was not far behind. After a discovery of gold on Hispaniola, the Spaniards forced the Arawaks to work the mines. They also enslaved some of the Indians, making them grow crops for the benefit of the settlers. In doing this, the Spanish rulers split up Arawak families ruthlessly, forcing fathers and mothers to leave their children to the not so tender mercies of alien masters. For the Arawaks, this was the final disaster. Harsh treatment, disease brought from Europe, and outright slaughter all but eradicated the Arawaks during the first third of the 16th century.

Before their disappearance from the scene, however, the Arawaks made a sizable impact on the colonizers. They introduced the Spaniards, and thus Europe, to crops such as potatoes, tobacco, peanuts, cassava, maize, pumpkins, and beans. They added words to the Spanish language such as "cacique" (chief), "bohío" (hut), "conuco" (maize field), and "guajiro" (a rude person). It is also a fair assumption that a good many early Spanish soldiers and settlers mated with Arawak women. Their descendants were gradually absorbed into the mainstream of Spanish colonial society.

The Caribs were not eliminated so easily or so totally. Faced with the superior weaponry of the Spaniards, they retreated to strongholds in the smaller, eastern Caribbean islands. The Spaniards did not pursue them. They were not much interested in the Lesser Antilles and they were not eager for pointless battles with the fierce Caribs. Many of the Caribs held out in the eastern Caribbean until the coming of the French and British to that part of the region in the 17th and 18th centuries. Stubborn as they were, the Caribs were also an anachronism and their near-extinction was inevitable. Today there are few people of Carib descent anywhere in the part of the world that bears their name.

Having established their sway over Hispaniola, the Spaniards set their sights on other parts of the Caribbean. In 1508 they built settlements in Puerto Rico; in 1509 they "pacified" the people of the Lucayan Islands, now the Bahamas, and moved into Jamaica; by 1511 the Spaniards had expanded their power to Cuba and Florida. Gold was discovered on Cuba, whereupon that island replaced Hispaniola as the center of attention in the growing Spanish empire in the New World. That lasted but a few years. When immense riches were discovered in Mexico and Peru, both Cuba and Hispaniola were reduced to the status of supply bases for the conquistadores on the mainland.

For more than a century after Columbus, Spain dominated the Caribbean. Its explorers, settlers, soldiers and priests seemed to be everywhere. But it was only a matter of time before other European powers, envious of Spain's empire in the Caribbean, began to challenge its monopoly of power. At first the British, French, and Dutch were content to encourage privateers such as Sir Francis Drake, Sir Walter Raleigh, and others to prey on Spanish shipping and plunder Spanish port cities in the Caribbean. Their appetites whetted, Britain, France, and the Netherlands then chartered companies to colonize in the region wherever it was economically and militarily feasible.

The newcomers did not challenge Spain's major Caribbean interests at first, concentrating instead on the smaller, marginal islands. The British successfully occupied Bermuda in 1612 and St. Kitts in 1624; soon afterward they took Barbados, Nevis, Antigua, and Barbuda. The French seized Martinique, Guadeloupe, and some other smaller islands. The Dutch installed themselves in Curaçao, Aruba, and Bonaire and also began the settlement of the Guianas.

The first Spanish settlement to fall in the Greater Antilles was Jamaica, which the British captured in 1655. Another British force sailed to the coast of Central America, defeated a small group of Spaniards and established what was to become British Honduras (now Belize). The French, in collaboration with some of the buccaneers who operated in the Caribbean, seized the western half of Hispaniola. Spain, unable to retake it, finally ceded it to France in 1697. It became the colony of Saint-Domingue, later Haiti.

As a result of military defeats in Europe, Spain was witnessing the beginning of the end of her global power and her unchallenged predominance in the Caribbean. Nonetheless, Spain clung to some of its major Caribbean possessions, and it would not be until the late 19th century that the Spanish flag disappeared from the region.

SUGAR AND SLAVES

Most of the original European settlers were small farmers, growing tobacco, ginger, indigo, and cotton for export, and maize, cassava, and vegetables for their own consumption. Labor in the fields was supplied chiefly by indentured servants brought from Europe. These workers, poor and discontented in their home countries, signed up for service in the colonies for a fixed period of time, usually five years. They were given room, board, and minimal wages; often they were badly treated. But when they fulfilled their contracts, most of them stayed on in the colonies, bought their own land, and imported their own indentured servants. The earliest indentured servants came voluntarily, but later, as the supply gradually dwindled, the European governments sent criminals and prisoners of war to maintain the labor supply.

Until the middle of the 17th century, tobacco was the most profitable export crop produced in the Caribbean colonies. An export crop is one produced primarily for sale abroad in exchange for the foreign currency required to buy imported goods. But as the better quality leaf from Virginia began to appear on the European market, tobacco growers in the Caribbean found it difficult to compete. Sugar cane, brought to the New World by Columbus, offered an alternative crop. The Portuguese had already established large sugar cane plantations in Brazil, and Dutch traders spread the word across the Caribbean about the Portuguese methods of extracting sugar from the cane. The French farmers in the Caribbean tried the new crop, then the British. It was an immediate success, since the temperature and rainfall were just right for sugar cane. Moreover, there was at the time an immense demand in Europe for sugar to sweeten coffee, tea, and cocoa, as well as for cakes, biscuits, and distilling rum.

The new crop created enormous social change wherever it was introduced. Since cane had to be made into sugar as soon as it was cut, each farmer had to have mills, boiling houses, and hauling animals of his own. These things were expensive, and a farmer could afford them only if he had enough land to plant many acres of cane and make great quantities of sugar. Poorer farmers, unable to do this, were forced to sell their land to their richer neighbors, and as a result small farms gave way to large plantations.

The cane growers quickly were confronted with a major problem: the shortage of labor. Cane growing required a large number of strong, unskilled workers. The Indians were no longer available and indentured servants from the home countries were largely city-bred, inept at agriculture, and inclined to rebelliousness. The solution to the labor shortage, the planters concluded, lay in Africa, where local chieftains were all too ready to sell their brethren into slavery. This "solution" was to have a tremendous impact on the future of the entire Caribbean region.

Even before the introduction of sugar cane as a major export crop, the Spaniards had brought slaves to the Caribbean. The earliest of them were Spanish-speaking blacks born in Spain, and by 1516 they outnumbered the white colonists in some Spanish territories. It was in 1518 that the first shipload of black slaves came directly from the west coast of Africa to the Spanish Caribbean, and from then on the trade flourished. In the Spanish territories, the slaves performed the physically demanding jobs of clearing forests, growing crops, tending animals, and working mines.

When the British and French colonies turned to slavery in the 17th century, it was—as we have seen—because of the revolutionary introduction of sugar cane and the need for great amounts of labor. As the transatlantic slave trade boomed, there developed what was called the "triangle of trade." The first side of the triangle consisted of the ships that carried cloth, whisky and cheap manufactures from northern Europe to the coast of West Africa. There they were exchanged for slaves, who had been provided to Portuguese and Dutch traders with posts along the coast. The second side of the triangle was the journey of the ships, now laden with terrified, shackled Africans, to the Caribbean. Once unchained, the slaves were auctioned off to planters on the spot and led away to a life of toil and humiliation in the canefields. The third leg of the trade triangle was the return of the ships to Europe, this time carrying cargoes of sugar, rum, and other tropical produce.

REVOLT IN THE CANEFIELDS

Few Europeans in the 16th and 17th centuries had scruples about the practice of slavery, and for the plantation owners of the Caribbean the African "black ivory" was a godsend. For the slaves, however, the wrenching transition from life in Africa to bondage in an alien land was a shocking experience. Families were torn apart, and many miserable men, women, and children died during the ocean voyage or from the brutal treatment they received in the New World.

Cut off from their homeland, most of the Africans reluctantly accepted their lot. But some rebelled against the life of slavery. New slaves would sometimes refuse proudly to work in the fields or come when they were summoned by a name bestowed on them by the master. Unable to conform to plantation life, many slaves chose an extreme form of protest, suicide. Seasoned slaves protested by working slowly, damaging tools, or poisoning animals and even overseers. Many simply ran away, mixing into free black groups in the cities or joining runaway-slave communities in the hinterlands. In the 17th and 18th centuries, slave revolts erupted frequently and were put down after heavy losses of life and property.

The most successful slave revolt of all came in Saint-Domingue, the French-ruled half of Hispaniola. There, at the end of the 18th century and in the early years of the 19th, black slaves led by Toussaint L' Ouverture rebelled against the planters and the French authorities. After years of bloody fighting, the blacks gained control of the country. The Emperor Napoleon dispatched troops to put down the rebellion, but the French, badly weakened by yellow fever, were unable to reestablish control and finally returned to France. The black leadership renamed the country Haiti, an Arawak word meaning "mountainous." It is ironic that the first independent state in the Caribbean was given an Amerindian name, not a European or African one.

EMANCIPATION

The last half of the 18th century saw the sugar colonies at the peak of their prosperity. From then on, Caribbean sugar declined. The slave labor force, with no incentive to work hard, was inefficient; the equipment was primitive; the planter class was far more interested in the good life than in production; and, most important, the competition of the newly developed sugar beet in Europe and North America meant large supplies of sugar and lower prices. The plantation and the planter class began to lose some of their former importance. As sugar became less profitable, planters experimented with other crops, but nothing proved quite so successful.

A happy consequence of the decline of sugar cane was that the weakened "plantocracy," as some writers have called the planter-dominated society, was unable to mount a strong fight against the growing anti-slavery sentiment in Europe. As the economic power of the planters waned, so did their political influence. Events moved swiftly. Britain abolished legal slavery in its colonies in 1838, the French and Danes followed in 1848, the Dutch in 1863, the Spanish in 1873 (Puerto Rico) and 1886 (Cuba).

Wherever they could, the emancipated slaves settled on small holdings of their own, particularly in territories where unused land was available. Many refused to work as free laborers in the canefields, to them a symbol of oppression. The free black peasant farmers bought the cheapest parcels of land and grew food crops that formerly were imported. Under the guidance of religious leaders and Europeans interested in their welfare, the ex-slaves formed agricultural cooperatives and "free villages"—communities where they could grow and sell their crops as a free peasantry no longer dominated by the plantation owners.

The emancipation of the slaves in the Caribbean created a severe labor shortage for the already hard-pressed sugar plantations, and so in the mid-19th century the region experienced a new wave of immigration. These newcomers were indentured laborers from Madeira, China, and India. Between 1838 and 1917, nearly a half a million Indians came to the Caribbean to work on the sugar estates. When their contracted period of work was over, most stayed on in the Caribbean and settled on small holdings of their own or began from scratch as businessmen. Today, the descendants of the indentured Asians form the majority of people in Guyana, the second largest group in Trinidad and Tobago, and a sizable percentage of the population in other Caribbean countries.

The experience of slavery had a profound influence on the Caribbean. Just how many Africans were shipped into bondage in the region is not known. But best estimates are that from two to five million blacks were brought across the Atlantic into slavery from the early 16th century until the slave trade was abolished. Today the descendants of those Africans who came in chains form the majority of people in most parts of the Caribbean.

CHAPTER 3

AMERICA ENTERS THE CARIBBEAN

It was only a matter of time before the United States became a factor in the Caribbean. The region, just to the south of the eastern seaboard, was a natural market for U.S. manufactures and a magnet for Yankee capital. It was inevitable that the United States, with its dynamism and ambition, would not only want to eject the Europeans from the Caribbean but replace them as the dominant power in the region.

TILTING WITH BRITAIN

After the United States successfully rebelled against Britain and became an independent country in 1783, its aggressive merchants and traders expanded their commercial interests wherever possible. Indeed, American attempts to cut into Britain's monopoly of trade with its Caribbean colonies was one of the causes of the War of 1812 between the United States and Britain. The British quite simply objected to upstart U.S. traders selling manufactured goods in the Caribbean in exchange for sugar and rum.

After the indecisive war, the British continued to prevent the sale of American goods carried in American ships in their Caribbean colonies. In response, the United States closed its ports to British ships sailing from Canada and the West Indies. After years of haggling, the conflict was resolved in 1830, when Britain decided to permit direct trade between the United States and the British colonies in the Caribbean. American merchants and shippers rejoiced as trade experienced a profitable boom.

As the United States grew in strength and confidence, it began to make it clear that the European presence in the Western Hemisphere was distinctly unwelcome. When the Spanish colonies in South and Central America revolted against the mother country in the first three decades of the 19th century, Americans supported the rebels and hailed their success. Most Americans applauded Kentucky's Henry Clay when he portrayed the Latin American revolutions as "the glorious spectacle of eighteen millions of people, struggling to burst their chains and be free."

After the former Spanish colonies became independent countries, trade between them and the United States multiplied, since Spanish trade regulations no longer applied. This economic interest, plus a popular American sympathy for democracy against despotism, created ardent support for the new republics to the south. As a result, when the vengeful king Ferdinand VII of Spain asked the monarchs of Austria, Prussia, France, and Russia to lend him ships and troops to regain his Latin American colonies, the United States let it be known that it would oppose such a move. Armed with the knowledge that he would have British support, President James Monroe decided to issue a "republican blast" of defiance at the monarchies of Europe. In a message to Congress, on December 2, 1823, Monroe warned the European powers—and not only Spain—against any attempt to interfere in "any portions of this hemisphere." The Monroe Doctrine, as it came to be called, stated:

The American continents . . . are henceforth not to be considered subjects for future colonization by European powers.

At the time, the United States probably did not have the military power to enforce its prohibition on "future" colonization in the hemisphere. But in this instance, British and American interests coincided. Just as the United States did not wish to see its Latin American markets closed off, the British also valued their trade with the Latin American republics. Moreover, Britain, by far the world's greatest naval power at the time, was opposed to rival European navies moving into the Caribbean. With Britain and its navy behind the Monroe Doctrine, the other Europeans decided to heed the American president's warning.

SPAIN'S FADING EMPIRE

In the early part of the 19th century, many American leaders cast covetous eyes on Cuba, the "Pearl of the Antilles." The reasons for this interest were various. Southern slaveowners, eager to add another slave state to the union, openly advocated seizing the fertile island. In this, they were supported by military men, who argued that Cuba was a logical place for a naval base to protect a Central American canal, if it were ever built. In 1854, President Franklin Pierce even offered to buy Cuba from Spain for $130 million, but public opinion in the north, fearful that Cuba would become another slave state, condemned the move. In any event, Spain rejected Pierce's offer and the issue of Cuba was shelved—for the time being.

After the Civil War, the United States experienced a major industrial boom. Railways expanded in all directions and oil, coal, and metals of all kinds were found in great abundance. American businessmen had no need to look abroad, and most Americans were far more interested in opening up the West than in dabbling in foreign countries. By the 1880s, however, that attitude began to change. Industrialists and bankers who made enormous profits in the United States now had surplus capital to invest, and so they began to look abroad for investment possibilities.

A particularly inviting area for U.S. business enterprise was the Spanish Caribbean. In the 1880s, American investors sank many millions of dollars into the Cuban sugar industry, buying plantations and factories and installing modern equipment. Soon American trade with the island reached $100 million a year. Moreover, the United States had replaced Spain as the biggest trading partner of Puerto Rico, Santo Domingo (now the Dominican Republic), and the Central American republics of El Salvador, Guatemala, and Honduras. By the 1890s, U.S. investment in the Caribbean and the neighboring mainland region amounted to 40 percent of the country's overseas investment.

Americans also took a keen interest in the independence movements that spang up in Puerto Rico, Santo Domingo, and Cuba. The once powerful Spanish empire was creaking with old age, but it nonetheless tried to cling to its remaining possessions in the Caribbean. Hoping to supplant Spanish colonial rule with democratic republics, idealistic Americans gave arms and money to the Caribbean rebels.

Santo Domingo was the first to gain independence. Actually, the Spanish were thrown out of the territory early in the century by the revolutionary Haitians, who occupied their Spanish-speaking neighbor and expelled the Spanish authorities. The Haitians remained until 1844, when local patriots rose up in arms, ejected the occupiers, and established an independent state named the Dominican Republic. But the country's troubles were far from over. In 1861 Spain reasserted her control over her former colony by sending troops to garrison it. But this caused loud complaints from the United States and led to a series of new rebellions by the Dominicans. The troublesome territory also proved to be a financial drain on Spain, and so in 1865 it withdrew its troops for good, leaving behind a second Dominican Republic.

In 1870, a group of Dominican leaders, anxious to bring order to their bankrupt and turbulent country, proposed that the United States annex it. Many business interests in the United States strongly favored the idea, and President Ulysses S. Grant was persuaded of the wisdom of annexation. But the American people responded coldly to the proposition and an annexation treaty was killed in the U.S. Senate. After that, the Dominican Republic drifted into confusion, disorder, and dictatorship. Its debts to European countries became so great that in the 1880s the Dominican government asked American bankers to take control of the country's customs service. Part of the money derived from customs duties went to pay off the foreign debt, thus averting an intervention by European armies in the Caribbean republic.

In Puerto Rico, the mid-1800s saw a number of revolts against Spanish rule, but all were put down easily by Spanish troops. Still, the independence movement continued to grow. Puerto Rican "independentistas" forged close ties to the liberal party in Spain, and Liberals promised to grant self-government to Puerto Rico should they ever come to power in Madrid. When the Liberals did gain control of the Spanish government in 1897, they were as good as their word. A new constitution granting Puerto Rico local self-rule, but not independence, was drawn up; in March, 1898, elections were held on the island that led to the formation of a government in July. All this, however, was to change as a result of the Spanish-American War.

WAR WITH SPAIN

Throughout the 19th century, small groups of Cubans had unfurled the flag of rebellion against Spanish rule. Time after time, Spanish troops squelched the uprisings. Finally, in 1895, an exiled Cuban patriot and writer, José Martí, returned to the island with his followers from their New York base and touched off a new revolt. Martí was killed in battle a few weeks later, but a bloody struggle, backed by Cubans of every class, soon spread across the island. Spain sent 200,000 troops to Cuba, but this time they could not contain the rebellion. As the U.S. press published lurid tales of Spanish atrocities, horrified Americans joined the rebel call for "Cuba Libre!"

Many Americans urged President William McKinley to intervene and stop the slaughter on America's doorstep. He hesitated, but he did dispatch the warship *Maine* to Cuban waters in January, 1898, to protect American citizens if that should become necessary. On February 15, 1898, two terrific explosions ripped the *Maine* apart, sending it to the bottom of Havana harbor with the loss of 266 lives.

The cause of the blasts was never clearly established, but Americans—goaded by jingoist newspapers—were quick to blame the Spanish authorities in Havana and their superiors in Madrid. As war fever spread from New England to California and the slogan of the hour became "Remember the *Maine!*" Assistant Secretary of the Navy Theodore Roosevelt won widespread acclaim by declaring that "we shall have this war for the freedom of Cuba."

Faced with the clamor for military action, McKinley abandoned his efforts toward a diplomatic solution with Spain and reluctantly signed a joint resolution of Congress declaring war. This was done on April 25, but not before Senator Henry M. Teller amended the resolution with the statement that the United States, once Cuba was free from Spain, would "leave the government and the control of the island to its people."

To the surprise of most Americans, the first action of the war took place in the Pacific. On May 1, battleships under the command of Commodore George Dewey steamed into Manila Bay and all but destroyed the Spanish fleet that was bottled up there. The Spanish naval base quickly surrendered, thousands of American troops were landed, and in August the Spanish formally handed over the Philippines to the United States.

Spanish resistance in Cuba, ineffectual as it was, was stiffer. A U.S. naval force blew Spain's Atlantic fleet out of the water as it tried to escape from Santiago harbor. Marines landed at Guantanamo and established the first American base on Cuban soil, while an army of some 17,000 U.S. soldiers landed near Santiago to the cheers of the Cubans. In the days that followed, American troops met fierce Spanish resistance outside Santiago, but Theodore Roosevelt's "Rough Riders" and a regiment of black cavalry* stormed up Kettle Hill and dislodged the defenders. Other U.S. troops seized nearby San Juan Hill after a bloody battle. Spanish resistance then crumbled rapidly, and by July 17 the Spanish flag, which had flown over Santiago for 384 years, was replaced by the Stars and Stripes.

In the meantime, another American force landed in Puerto Rico and seized the island after token Spanish opposition. On August 12, less than four months after the war began, Spain agreed to a ceasefire. Under the Treaty of Paris, signed in December, Spain handed over the Philippines, Guam, and Puerto Rico to the Americans. It was agreed that the U.S. Army would remain in Cuba until a suitable civilian government was established.

NEW ERA IN THE CARIBBEAN

As a result of the "splendid little war," as U.S. diplomat John Hay described it, the United States became a major Caribbean power in the early years of the 20th century.

---

*One of the cavalry's officers was Capt. John J. Pershing, later to become commander of the American troops in Europe during World War I.

After a short period of U.S. military government, Congress gave Puerto Rico a civilian government, including a lower house made up of elected Puerto Ricans. But Americans ruled the roost. The powerful upper house was composed of an American governor and five "official" members appointed by the U.S. government. Congress established a Puerto Rican Supreme Court, but its judges were appointed by the United States. To improve the conditions of the Puerto Rican people, armies of U.S. doctors, engineers, and technicians roamed the island, carrying out the good work of fighting disease, building roads, and repairing harbors.

Cuba at first was ruled by American military governors, who, as in Puerto Rico, established construction and health care projects. The Cubans welcomed the Yankee paternalism at first, but after a few years they began to complain about the military occupation and remind the United States of the promise of independence made in the Teller Amendment to the resolution declaring war against Spain.

Accordingly, the United States handed over the government to the Cubans in 1902, and in the same year Tomás Estrada Palma was elected as the first president of free Cuba. The country inherited a democratic constitution from the Americans, but, at U.S. insistence, it included the so-called Platt Amendment. This gave the United States the right to oversee Cuba's foreign policy, intervene in its internal affairs if it thought fit, and maintain naval bases on the island, like the one later established at Guantanamo.

In 1901, President McKinley was assassinated and Vice President Theodore Roosevelt succeeded him. He then was elected to a full term in the White House from 1904 to 1908, and in his seven years in office Teddy Roosevelt paid particular heed to events in the Caribbean and its environs. In 1902, when Britain and Germany sent gunboats to Venezuela in an attempt for force that country to pay its debts, Roosevelt—alarmed at the possibility that the Europeans would occupy Venezuela—warned that the United States would send troops to the area unless an agreement was reached. Both the British and the Germans quickly agreed to arbitrate their differences with Venezuela. Roosevelt's warning had reestablished the Monroe Doctrine as a continuing American policy that Europeans could not flout unless they wished to risk conflict with the United States.

The next year, Roosevelt again took forceful action, this time in connection with the proposed canal through the Panamanian isthmus. At the time, the territory belonged to Colombia, which had rejected U.S. terms for a treaty allowing the United States to proceed with the digging. Roosevelt was annoyed with the Colombians, and so when a small group of Panamanians declared independence from Colombia the U.S. president was quick to back them up. First he sent a cruiser to the area, ostensibly to "keep order" but in reality to prevent Colombian troops from landing and crushing the revolt. Then the United States quickly recognized the independent state of Panama; within a week a treaty was signed authorizing the start of work on the canal. "I took Panama," Roosevelt later boasted. "It was the only way the canal could be constructed."

THE ROOSEVELT COROLLARY

Roosevelt made it bluntly clear that the United States would play a policeman's role in the Caribbean and Central America. He was convinced that the "insurrectionary habit" of the "wretched republics" of the area imposed certain obligations on Washington. In a speech to Congress in 1904, he declared that the United States would adhere to the Monroe Doctrine and not allow European countries to interfere in the Western Hemisphere. But then he added what came to be known as the Roosevelt Corollary to the Monroe Doctrine:

Chronic wrongdoing . . . may in America, as elsewhere, ultimately require intervention by some civilized nation, and in the Western Hemisphere the adherence of the United States to the Monroe Doctrine may force the United States, however reluctantly, in flagrant cases of such wrongdoing or impotence, to the exercise of an international police power.

In other words, the Monroe Doctrine, originally designed to prevent intervention by European powers, would be used to justify intervention by the United States. As policeman of the hemisphere, the United States intervened frequently over the next few decades. In 1905, Roosevelt used the threat of military force to make the chaotic Dominican Republic accept an American designated by him as its customs collector. The customs duties collected were used to pay off European and American creditors. Woodrow Wilson also felt it necessary to intervene in the Dominican Republic, for far different reasons. In 1916, on the eve of America's entry into World War I, the Dominican Republic was in the throes of an insurrection. President Wilson was informed that German agents hoped to take advantage of the chaos and establish a pro-German country in the Caribbean. Faced with this intolerable possibility, Wilson sent in the United States Marines. They quickly restored order and installed an American military government that was to last eight years.

Cuba, where the United States had large economic interests and which was regarded as a vital part of the U.S. defense system, also grew used to seeing American troops. When President Tomás Estrada Palma won reelection in 1906, his opponents accused him of stealing the election and demanded his overthrow. As disorder spread, Estrada Palma himself asked the United States to restore order. President Roosevelt sent U.S. troops to Cuba, but he also sent a personal friend, Charles Magoon, to administer the country. In this period, U.S. influence in Cuba expanded rapidly as Americans poured in to represent mainland bankers and companies and to administer their Cuban investments. In 1909, to the surprise of many in Europe who thought the United States had taken Cuba for good, Magoon supervised a new election and handed over power to the second president, José Miguel Gómez. U.S. troops were withdrawn, but they were sent back in 1917 and again in 1921, when American presidents perceived that chaos on the island was damaging to U.S. interests.

Successive governments in Haiti were so weak and corrupt that it was not difficult for American bankers, in the early years of the 20th century, to gain control of the country's national bank, railways, public utilities, and customs houses. Between 1908 and 1915, seven different men seized the presidency in Port-au-Prince, and when the First World War broke out in 1914 Germany saw unstable Haiti as a possible supply base for use against Britain and its allies. When Kaiser Wilhelm II, the German ruler, threatened to seize Haiti for nonpayment of debts, President Wilson acted decisively, sending the marines to occupy the country. Americans were put in charge of the customs service, the treasury and police; they also established health and public works projects. The Haitians were forced to accept a new constitution, which among other things allowed white foreigners to own land, something forbidden since the days of Toussaint L'Ouverture. The intervention, which began as a move to block German strategy during the war and guard the approaches of the recently opened Panama Canal, was to last until 1934.

In the decades after President Roosevelt assumed the policeman's role for the United States, American troops also intervened in Central America. Honduras was occupied briefly in the 1920s; Nicaragua, constantly in a state of insurrection, and always in debt to European bankers, suffered three Yankee occupations between 1909 and 1933.

AMERICAN POSSESSIONS

Neither Teddy Roosevelt nor his successors had need to send troops to Puerto Rico. They were there already. After the Spanish-American War, the island was a possession of the United States. It was ruled by an American governor; the members of its upper house and Supreme Court were chosen in Washington. Naturally enough, many Puerto Ricans resented this, and to still dissent Congress passed the Jones Act in 1917. This law granted U.S. citizenship to Puerto Ricans, with full freedom to live on the mainland or on the island. Under the Jones Act, both the upper and lower legislative houses were to be locally elected. Nevertheless, real power still resided with the American governor and his executive council. The governor was able to veto budget items passed by the legislature, and the U.S. Congress and the U.S. president could disallow any law enacted by the Puerto Ricans.

Another special case was that of the tiny Danish colonies of St. Thomas, St. John, and St. Croix. Occupying a strategic position in the eastern Caribbean, these Danish Virgin Islands had been regarded for some time by the U.S. Navy as a possible first line of defense against an attack from the Atlantic on the Panama Canal. America's entry into World War I against Germany increased the navy's appetite for the Danish colonies, and—after the U.S. told Denmark that American troops might seize the islets to prevent a German takeover—the Danes sold them for $25 million. The islands were renamed the U.S. Virgin Islands.

GOOD NEIGHBORS

After World War I, American attitudes toward the Caribbean began to change. No longer was there a risk of European intervention in the Western Hemisphere, since defeated Germany was powerless and Britain and France, weakened by the war, could not afford to displease the

United States. In short, defense was not a plausible reason for intervention any longer. Moreover, U.S. leaders had become aware that paternalistic interference by the *yanqui* colossus, no matter how well intentioned, was viewed with loathing throughout the Caribbean and Latin America.

Accordingly, during the 1920s and 1930s, American governments reduced direct military and political involvement in the Caribbean region. Presidents Warren Harding and Calvin Coolidge all but repudiated the Roosevelt Corollary justifying America's police role. President Herbert Hoover took office in 1929 vowing to accelerate "the retreat from imperialism" in the Caribbean. Hoover, determined to keep American hands out of the internal affairs of the countries to the south, coined the phrase "Good Neighbor" to describe his policy. Hoover's phrase and policy was adopted by his successor, Franklin D. Roosevelt, who vigorously opposed the kind of interventionism earlier advocated by his distant cousin, Theodore.

The change in policy led to the withdrawal of U.S. troops from the Dominican Republic, Nicaragua, and Haiti. As of the early 1930s, the only American troops remaining in the Caribbean region were in Puerto Rico, the Virgin Islands, and—in accord with treaty provisions—the Panama Canal Zone and Guantanamo Naval Base, Cuba.

The Good Neighbor Policy eliminated—until later in the century—the most objectionable aspects of U.S. dealings in the Caribbean. But, if anything, it led to a strengthening of American economic influence in the area. By the 1930s, American stockholders controlled sugar in Cuba and the Dominican Republic, utilities and banking in many places, and bananas wherever they were grown. The Yankee troops had gone home, but Yankee businessmen still played key roles in the economies of countries throughout the Caribbean. Moreover, the departing American soldiers left behind governments which all too often turned out to be repressive and corrupt.

The 19th century and the early decades of the 20th century had witnessed enormous changes in the Caribbean. Britain, France, and the Netherlands retained their colonies, but Spain—once the dominant power in the region—was forced to withdraw to the Old World. The United States became a major political and economic force in the Caribbean and, for a time, assumed the role of its policeman. The the era of rampant American interventionism gave way to the Good Neighbor approach. This would prevail until World War II, an event that was to prove a significant watershed for the countries of the Caribbean.

CHAPTER ■4■ WINDS OF CHANGE

The spirit of nationalism and the passion for independence that swept across the Spanish-speaking Caribbean in the 19th century did not spread to other parts of the region at that time. But it was inevitable that the old colonial structures in the British, French, and Dutch sectors of the Caribbean would also feel the winds of change. When they did, in the early and middle decades of the 20th century, each colonial power bent before those winds in a different way. The United States, the newest power in the Caribbean, also had to make adjustments, particularly in its relationship with Puerto Rico.

CROWN COLONY GOVERNMENT

Up until 1865, most of the British colonies in the Caribbean had locally elected assemblies composed of leading planters, merchants, and lawyers. The vote was restricted to a very small number of property-owning males, almost all of them white. These assemblies did not have much power, but they could, and often did, obstruct programs favored by the British governor and the Colonial Office in London. In 1838, for example, the Jamaican assembly, angered by a law enacted by the British parliament that would transfer authority of the island's prison system from local magistrates to the governor, refused to pass the annual law giving the governor the power to collect taxes and maintain law and order.

The British Colonial Office was determined to do away with the troublesome assemblies. For one thing, they represented a small, rich, privileged class. For another, they were notorious for their mistreatment of the newly emancipated blacks, who often were prevented from buying land. In 1865, after rioting by black farmers, the Jamaican authorities summarily executed as many as 600 of them and flogged hundreds more. In Britain, many influential people were horrified at the brutality and the government decided that the time had come to take a stronger hand in ruling the colonies. This was to be done by crown colony rule. Under crown colony government, all power was concentrated in the hands of representatives of the British Crown. The assemblies were dissolved and near-total power was given to the governors and their apponted executive councils.

After some pressure, Jamaica became the first to accept the crown colony system in 1865, and in the years that followed almost every one of the British colonies in the Caribbean was brought under the same form of government. As a result, the power of the local upper classes was greatly curtailed and free blacks were given a greater measure of justice. There were, however, drawbacks to crown colony rule. By shutting local people out of positions of authority, the system was poor preparation for the self-government that eventually was to come to the Caribbean.

Crown colony government lasted into the 20th century. Some of the wealthier local people did serve on town councils at the discretion of the governor, and some of them were influential advisors. But the wealthier upper classes wanted a return to the elected assemblies, and in this they were joined by the British Caribbean's growing middle class. This middle class was composed of small merchants and professionals, chiefly townspeople; most were white Europeans but some were of mixed race. They sought a share in government and a right to vote—but only for themselves, not for blacks or poor whites. They strenuously opposed black self-help societies, which they claimed were deliberate attempts to set class against class, blacks against whites.

In the 1920s and 1930s the British government sent commission after commission to the Caribbean to study the complaints of the local people. But little was accomplished and it was clear that the demands of the middle class for limited political change had not produced results. At the same time, black leaders and labor leaders, who were chiefly black and colored (racially mixed), were making demands of their own. They wanted far more fundamental changes in the system of government in the British Caribbean, and these changes included elective government, votes for every adult regardless of wealth, race, or sex, and a large amount of local self-government.

THE RISE OF LABOR

Throughout the 1920s and 1930s, the British Caribbean experienced the rise of labor unions as a political force. Many of the new union leaders had worked in Britain and the United States during World War I and had become active in union affairs. Others had fought in the British army and believed they had earned the right to raise their voices for political reform in the colonies. During the war, when trade with Britain had been curtailed, Caribbean businessmen greatly increased the manufacture of local goods. These new industries created a body of working class people in the cities of the British Caribbean, and the new urban workers became natural recruits for the post-war unions.

All through the 1920s, the fledgling unions had to battle for the legal right to exist. Laws on the books in most colonies at the time enabled the authorities to charge anyone who organized workers with illegal conspiracy. Some laws forbade picketing at the workplace; others permitted employers to sue unions for business losses suffered during a strike. But pressure from the British government and support from the British Labour party gradually helped the Caribbean unions to win legal status and a widely accepted role in the colonial economies. Moreover, the union leaders began to form labor parties modeled after the British Labour party, and to demand radical changes in the crown colony system, not in the name of the privileged but in the name of the common people.

The Depression years of the early 1930s were a time of low wages, unemployment, and misery for workers in the British Caribbean. Strikes, hunger marches, and riots flared up everywhere, initially in the smaller islands, then in Jamaica, Trinidad, and Barbados. At first the governors made a show of force, calling in marines, warships, and armed police under British commanders. But nothing was done to address the fundamental causes of the unrest, and so the disturbances went on, often with bloody consequences.

Back in London, Britons were stunned by the disorder sweeping through the colonies. Few were aware of the desperate condition of the the Caribbean poor and of the sorry state of the colonial economies. Most of these economies were still geared to growing crops for export to the United States and Europe. Insufficient attention had been given to the development of local industry, or to crops diversified enough to meet local consumption needs. It was an amazing fact that a large percentage of the food consumed on these largely agricultural islands—including milk and meat—had to be imported and therefore was priced beyond the reach of many.

THE MOYNE COMMISSION

As a result of the labor riots, the British government continued to send investigatory commissions to the Caribbean, and some of them reported that the unrest was due to the dismal poverty afflicting a large number of people on the islands. The last and most important of these commissions was headed by Lord Moyne in the late 1930s. The members of the Moyne Commission visited each colony and talked to people of every class, color, and occupation. They probed every aspect of economic life and social conditions, including health, housing, and education. They also heard arguments for and against self-government, elections with universal adult suffrage, and a linking of the territories into an English-speaking Caribbean federation.

Lord Moyne's report to the British government was a strong condemnation of the policies that allowed hunger, disease, unemployment, and misery to exist as they did in the Caribbean colonies. The full report was not published until the end of 1944, when victory in World War II was in sight, but—to its credit—the British government acted on some of Lord Moyne's proposals even as German bombs were falling on London in 1940 and 1941. Public works programs were established in the colonies as a temporary answer to unemployment. A special fund was set up to help with economc and social projects in all the poorer parts of the empire, and a Colonial Development and Welfare Organization (CDWO) charged with administering the program was established. The Caribbean branch of the CDWO was located in Barbados. In accord with Lord Moyne's recommendations, the Colonial Office also sent a memorandum to all colonial governments instructing them to remove legal obstacles to union activity. In addition, some of the colonies were told to draw up programs for workmen's compensation, unemployment insurance, and minimum wages.

To the more militant Caribbean leaders, a disappointing aspect of Lord Moyne's report was its lukewarm reaction to their political objectives. Where they hoped for a ringing endorsement, the report called for a "cautious extension" of the franchise, "eventual" self-government, and further study of the "long-term" goal of federation. But the political and social dynamics generated by World War II quickly rendered Lord Moyne's political caution out of date. Anxious to rally as much support as possible behind the war against Nazi Germany and the rest of the Axis, the wartime British government, headed by Winston Churchill, began to talk about "partnership" among the peoples of the British Empire. It also stated openly for the first time that it planned to replace crown colony rule in the Caribbean with freely elected governments.

SELF-GOVERNMENT
AND FEDERATION

Britain's commitment to self-government in the Caribbean was strengthened by the victory of the Labour party in the postwar elections of 1945. Members of the new government were longtime sympathizers with the labor and nationalist movements in the empire. Still, even the Labour government of Clement Attlee offered only "self-government" and not outright "independence." Step by step, British governments after World War II granted the Caribbean colonies universal adult suffrage and full internal self-government. But the Colonial Office in London retained control over the islands' defense and foreign policies, and British governors—who retained the power to remove elected governments—remained behind in the Caribbean to keep watch over events.

In most of the colonies, union-based political parties

committed to full independence either ran the government or formed a strong opposition. The British, however, were not convinced that independence for each of the colonies was a practical thing, and argued that the territories should be combined in a federation before full independence could be discussed. Many Caribbean leaders agreed with the British that federation should come first, and in the post-World War II era there even seemed a fair chance of success in forging such a federation of English-speaking Caribbean territories. In the past, the major opposition to federation had come from the old wealthy classes, who feared that the influence they wielded in a small community would be diluted in a larger one. But by the mid-20th century their power had waned. Multinational businesses were moving into the region, and these powerful interests favored a regional approach to production and marketing. Some labor leaders, envisaging one powerful union throughout the British Caribbean, gave strong support to the drive for federation.

In an attempt to construct a federation, the Colonial Office held conferences in 1947, 1953, 1955, and 1956. Most of those in attendance, leaders from all parts of the British Caribbean, favored some sort of federation. But there was a wide range of opinion on particulars. Some favored a strong federal government with the power to enact laws and overrule the territories if their laws came into conflict. Some also wanted the federal government to have control over taxation and migration, a touchy issue in an area where the unemployed traditionally have sought to move from island to island in search of work. But other Caribbean leaders strongly objected to giving a federal government such substantial power, and in the end their views largely prevailed. It was finally agreed that in the first five years of its existence the West Indies Federation would have only three major tasks: to administer the distribution of CDWO funds; to support the West India Regiment; and to develop the University of the West Indies.

The federal government would have no real authority over the individual islands and it would not have the power to tax. Instead, it would be financed by fixed payments from each territory.

After years of hot debate, it was decided that the seat of the West Indies Federation would be Trinidad. The legislative branch would be a forty-five-member Assembly, with seats distributed as follows: Jamaica, seventeen; Trinidad and Tobago, ten; Barbados, five; the smaller islands would share the rest. Elections to the Assembly, contested by political leaders from all over the British Caribbean, were held on March 25, 1958. The West Indies Federal Labour party (WIFLP), a coalition of democratic socialist groups, won twenty-two seats and became the Assembly's largest party. An alliance of more conservative parties called the Democratic Labour party (DLP) won twenty seats, and independents the remaining three. With the support of the independents, the WIFLP was able to form a shaky government: the first prime minister of the West Indies Federation was an Oxford graduate and lawyer, Sir Grantley Adams of Barbados.

Adams faced a difficult predicament. Britain still controlled foreign policy and defense, so the federation had little standing in the world community. Moreover, the federation was to have no power over taxation, customs collections, or the migration of people for the first five years of its existence. The Barbadian's task was to keep the jerry-built federation alive for five years in hopes of building confidence in the new system and acquiring more power for the central government.

The task proved to be impossible. Norman Manley, chief minister in Jamaica, and Eric Williams, chief minister in Trinidad, leaders of the two most populous and economically viable territories, had vastly different views on the future of federalism. Williams wanted to move quickly to create a much stronger federation, with wide powers of taxation, a customs union to collect duties for all members, and a national bank. He wanted the federal government to gain control over education as well as such services as radio, transportation, and the post office. On the other hand, Manley, though a federalist at heart, was under strong anti-federalist pressure on Jamaica, where many people preferred the idea of independence as a separate state. As a result, he began to demand permanent restriction of the federal government's power to collect taxes and customs. Manley also insisted that the federal Assembly be changed so that seats be awarded on the basis of population, an arrangement that would have given Jamaica a permanent majority over the rest of the territories combined.

Prime Minister Adams tried to bring Williams and Manley closer together, but neither would budge. Manley then decided to hold a referendum as a test of public opinion on federation. In September 1961, a solid majority of Jamaicans voted to withdraw from the federation. With that, Manley asked that Jamaica be admitted into the British Commonwealth as a fully independent nation. Williams, convinced that federation had received a mortal wound ("ten minus one is zero," he said), announced that Trinidad, too, would withdraw and seek full independence.

INDEPENDENCE

In August 1962, both Jamaica and Trinidad and Tobago were admitted to the Commonwealth as fully independent states. They soon became the English-speaking Caribbean's first members of the United Nations. Attempts to retain the federal structure without Jamaica and Trinidad and Tobago dragged on for a few years and then were quietly abandoned. The West Indies Federation was dead. In November 1966, Barbados became independent, and in the 1970s and 1980s other British Caribbean territories made the same decision. Grenada (1974), Dominica (1978), St. Vincent-Grenadines (1979), Antigua and Barbuda (1981), and St. Kitts-Nevis (1983) became independent, democratic mini-states, with membership in the British Commonwealth and the United Nations.

Other British colonies in the Caribbean had chosen at the start not to join in the West Indies Federation. They also were granted full independence: Guyana in 1966, the Bahamas in 1973, Belize in 1981. As of 1984, a number of other territories remained at their own request under British control. These included Anguilla, the British Virgin Islands, the Cayman Islands, and the Turks and Caicos Islands.

THE DUTCH COLONIES

The Dutch colonies in the Caribbean, dating back to the 17th century, usually have been divided into three groups: those in the Leeward Islands (St. Eustatius, Saba and St. Maarten), those in the Windward Islands (Aruba, Curaçao and Bonaire), and mainland Suriname. Over the centuries, these colonies developed assemblies, or "statens," dominated by planters and merchants. A governor appointed in Holland presided over the seven colonies; the system prevailed until well into the 20th century.

By 1900, the six island colonies—once reasonably prosperous trade centers and slave markets—were struggling to survive. All had poor soil, inadequate water supplies, and overly large populations. In the years since then, little has changed in the three tiny islands in the Leewards and in Bonaire. But Royal Dutch Shell's discovery of oil in Venezuela in 1914 was to have a tremendous impact on Aruba and Curaçao. Because of Venezuela's unstable politics at the time, Shell was unwilling to spend large sums to build refineries there, and so it chose to locate them on the Dutch islands off the coast. By the 1930s, the oil company had several large refineries on Curaçao and one on Aruba; a subsidiary of Standard Oil also operated a huge refinery on Aruba. The refineries provided many thousands of jobs, attracting migrants from all over the Caribbean. As a result, the population of Curaçao and Aruba expanded swiftly, as did the size of their cities and towns. By the 1950s, the two islands enjoyed living standards that were among the highest in the Caribbean.

The new economic conditions inevitably created a new political atmosphere. A rising middle class of refinery employees and merchants began to challenge the old colonial system, forming political parties and clamoring for home rule. Adapting quickly to the new conditions, the Netherlands granted Curaçao and Aruba universal adult suffrage and internal self-government in 1949. Going even further, in 1954 the Dutch concocted a scheme whereby the Caribbean territories were made partners in a tripartite kingdom. The three members of the one kingdom were the Dutch Caribbean islands, Suriname, and the Netherlands. Each was to have full internal self-government; foreign affairs were to be a "joint responsibility."

Like the attempt at federation in the British Caribbean, the tripartite kingdom did not last long. Nationalist politicians argued that such close institutional ties with the Netherlands would hinder the development of a distinct Caribbean identity, and they pointed out that the greater wealth and influence of the Netherlands would assure its dominance in foreign policy decisions. Moreover, after an oil workers' demonstration erupted into violence in 1969, Dutch paratroops were rushed in to restore order. Nationalists in the Dutch Caribbean saw this as proof that the tripartite kingdom was merely a political facade, behind which control still remained in the hands of the Dutch.

Nationalist sentiment remained strong in the Dutch West Indies in the 1970s, but as of 1984 the islands remained under the control of the Netherlands. Mainland Suriname, which possessed rich bauxite deposits and vast forestry reserves, had a stronger case for full independence and made it more forcefully. It withdrew from the tripartite kingdom in 1975 and, after brief negotiations with the Dutch, became an independent republic with a freely elected parliament. The Dutch government agreed to provide $1.5 billion in economic assistance to the new country over its first fifteen years of independence.

THE FRENCH COLONIES

In the early 19th century, the French colonies—Martinique, Guadeloupe, and French Guiana—had nothing resembling the assemblies that existed in the British and Dutch Caribbean. The French colonies were governed by officials appointed by the French government in Paris. On a local level, however, mayors and other officials were elected, at first by a very limited number of men. From 1848 onward, however, all adult males in the French colonies had the right to vote. This meant that the blacks who were emancipated in 1843 had a strong voice in these local elections. Moreover, they and the other colonials could vote for the three deputies that each colony was allowed to send to the National Assembly in Paris.

These policies created strong ties of allegiance between the French colonies and France itself, and as a result anticolonialist feelings were less widespread than in other parts of the Caribbean. The French possessions were staunch supporters of France during two world wars, in which colonials fought alongside Frenchmen. After World War II, when France offered its colonies the choice of independence or amalgamation with France, the French colonies in Africa chose independence. On the other hand, the Caribbean territories, Martinique, Guadeloupe, and French Guiana, as well as the Indian Ocean island of Réunion, chose amalgamation with France.

The French Government accepted these decisions. The African countries, though independent, chose to retain close economic and cultural ties with France. In 1946, the Caribbean territories became departments of France, with the same rights and privileges as the ninety departments in France itself. Colonial governors were replaced by prefects appointed in Paris, just as in the mainland departments. Each of the overseas departments was given the right to elect deputies for the French National Assembly and Senate. On the local level, general councils were established, first merely to advise the prefect, later with expanded powers, including some control over the spending of government investment funds.

The creation of the overseas departments quickly led to the formation of political parties and to hotly contested elections for the general councils and for the National Assembly and Senate. The parties aligned themselves with parties in France that shared similar political viewpoints. Conservatives and moderates generally favored the idea of being full-fledged departments of France, while left-wing parties argued for a much greater degree of local autonomy, including lawmaking powers for the councils. The Communist party, which had strong support in Martinique and Guadeloupe, denounced departmentalization as just another form of colonialism and demanded complete independence. In this they were joined by literary intellectuals, who believed that the closeness of the bonds with France was stifling Afro-Caribbean culture.

Supporters of departmentalization, on the other hand, point to its economic benefits. As departments of France, the former colonies share in French treasury funds for roads, health, education, and housing. Their citizens are entitled to social security, unemployment benefits, and health benefits. And since France is a member of the European Economic Community, agricultural products from Martinique, Guadeloupe, and French Guiana are allowed into western Europe at the same low customs rates as products from France.

PROGRESS IN PUERTO RICO

The Great Depression of the 1930s was a severe blow to Puerto Rico. As Americans tightened their belts, exports from Puerto Rico to the mainland slumped badly. Cigar and cigarette factories had to shut their doors, and thousands of sugar workers lost their jobs when the U.S. Congress ordered Puerto Rican sugar production cut in half. After Franklin D. Roosevelt was elected president in 1932, he launched the New Deal, a vast program designed to provide temporary relief to those badly hurt by the Depression and to get the crippled American economy on its feet again. As part of this program, huge amounts of money flowed from the U.S. treasury into social programs such as social security and unemployment benefits, and into public works projects that built roads, dams and public housing. The program was also applied to Puerto Rico, where it was called the "Little New Deal."

Before long, one third of Puerto Rico's workforce was earning wages from the public works programs. But if the Little New Deal saw Puerto Rico through the worst of the Depression, it did not deal with the fundamental problems that Puerto Rico shared with the rest of the Caribbean—a dependence on export crops, large amounts of unused land held by absentee owners, and no local industry to speak of.

As a consequence, progressive Puerto Rican politicians like Luis Muñoz Marin called for a thorough overhauling of the island's economy, with an emphasis on land reform and the encouragement of local industry. Muñoz Marin's Popular Democratic Party won the elections of 1940 and he became president of the Senate and head of the Puerto Rican government. Roosevelt approved of Muñoz Marin's plans and appointed as governor Rexford Guy Tugwell, a man who also supported them. Between them, Muñoz Marin and Tugwell set about remaking Puerto Rico in a program later called "Operation Bootstrap."

It must be remembered that the Puerto Rican government at that time was under the constant scrutiny of the U.S. Congress, which could overrule any of the actions taken on the island. So Muñoz Marin mixed daring and caution. His government did not attempt to expropriate large amounts of privately owned land. But it did take over failing sugar plantations and operate them under profit-sharing arrangements with the workers. New crops, such as pineapples, were grown on government lands, and then the seeds and know-how were made available to private planters. Experimental farms were established for beef and dairy cattle and pigs and chickens, and small farmers were encouraged to learn from the experiments. As a result, the production of beef, dairy products, and vegetables rose sharply; by 1958 they brought in about a half of the Puerto Rican farmer's earnings, a marked change from the almost total dependence on export crops such as tobacco, coffee, and sugar.

Muñoz Marin was also determined to improve the lot of the lower-rung agricultural worker. Landless farmers were sold small plots of government-owned land at low prices and with many years to pay. Small farmers were helped with loans and with expert advice on how to set up credit unions, co-operative stores, and rural schools. For the first time, electricity was brought to the countryside, where it illuminated homes and energized small businesses. Thatched huts were replaced by solid homes provided at cost by the government so long as the buyers donated their labor to help build them. By the early 1950s, many thousands of poor farmers lived in houses they had bought and paid for and could call their own.

Agriculture was important, but Muñoz Marin was convinced that Puerto Rico's rapidly rising population would never enjoy an adequate standard of living unless it developed new industries. At first the government built a small number of factories and plants to make products out of local raw materials. But these government-owned industries had little success, and so the pragmatic Muñoz Marin switched gears and began to emphasize government aid to private enterprise. Companies willing to open factories in Puerto Rico were exempt from paying taxes on their profits for ten years. The government even helped prospective entrepreneurs find sites and construct factories. Sometimes the Puerto Rican government made loans to finance new ventures. As more and more companies from the United States and elsewhere took advantage of the favorable economic climate, the Puerto Rican government began to train workers for the new industries.

Many of the new factories made clothes and shoes; others processed food, assembled electrical products and machinery, produced chemicals and metals. By the mid-1950s, manufacturing and processing earned more for the island in terms of exports than did agriculture—an extraordinary reversal of the usual pattern in the Caribbean. The industrialization generated hundreds of thousands of new jobs, resulting in an increase of per capita income from $279 in 1950 to $1,129 in 1968. Throughout the Caribbean, governments and political leaders were impressed by the success of Muñoz Marin's policy of throwing out the welcome mat for foreign capital.

The new wealth also meant more tax revenues for the government, and successive Muñoz Marin governments invested huge amounts in social welfare programs and public works. Power plants were built, new schools were opened, free lunch programs were begun. Illiteracy fell to less than 15 percent in 1970; life expectancy leaped from forty-six years in 1940 to seventy years in 1970. Puerto Rico still had its problems, including a stubbornly high rate of unemployment, but it was impossible to deny that Operation Bootstrap had achieved major gains for the island.

A NEW RELATIONSHIP

The winds of change also affected Puerto Rico's political status. When Tugwell resigned as governor in 1946, he persuaded President Harry Truman to appoint a Puerto

Rican, Jesús T. Piñero, as interim governor for two years. In 1947 Congress amended the Jones Act to provide that future governors of Puerto Rico be elected, not appointed by the U.S. president. Next year, Muñoz Marin became the first elected governor of the island.

Losing no time, Muñoz Marin immediately set about winning a change in Puerto Rico's fundamental political relationship with the United States. He wanted the island to be completely self-governing in its domestic affairs, leaving foreign affairs and defense to the United States. Moreover, he proposed that Puerto Rico become a commonwealth, no longer under the direct control of the United States but "freely associated" with it. Congress was divided on the issue, but in 1949 it voted to permit the election of a convention to prepare a new constitution for Puerto Rico. The delegates to the convention wrote a document calling for full internal self-government plus free association with the United States. It also called for an elected government, a two-house legislature and a multi-party system. Congress accepted the new constitution, and in 1952 the people of Puerto Rico solidly backed it in a plebiscite.

Muñoz Marin retired in 1964, and since then a number of Puerto Rican politicians have accused him of excessive caution. Some of them would like to see Puerto Rico become the fifty-first state in the United States; others fight—sometimes violently—for total independence. A small terrorist organization known as the Armed Forces of National Liberation (FALN) from time to time has staged murderous bombings to publicize its demand for an independent, left-wing Puerto Rico. But its violent activities have made little impact on the people of Puerto Rico. A referendum in 1967 showed that 60 percent of Puerto Rican voters favored the retention of commonwealth status. A sizable minority voted for statehood, while a very small percentage chose outright independence. In 1980, governor Carlos Romero Barceló, leader of the New Progressive party, was elected to a second term in office. The New Progressive party, allied with the Republican party in the United States, favored statehood. But Romero's margin of victory over the candidate of a party favoring commonwealth status was so slender that the governor decided not to press his campaign for statehood. The issue of Puerto Rico's status seemed certain to remain heated throughout the 1980s and perhaps beyond.

CHAPTER 5
CASTRO AND COMMUNISM

The Cuban revolution began inauspiciously, with a suicidal attack by a small band of young men and women on the Moncada military barracks in Santiago de Cuba in 1953. The attack failed miserably. But its leader, Fidel Castro, survived and later led the guerrilla army that toppled a brutal dictatorship in Cuba, replacing it with another kind of repression. Castro's revolution brought the first Communist state to the Caribbean, an event that would have tremendous significance for the region, for Latin America as a whole, and for the United States.

THE BATISTA YEARS

To understand the Castro revolution it is necessary to step back and have a look at Cuba's unhappy history during earlier decades of the century. In 1933, the conduct of Cuban dictator Gerardo ("the Butcher") Machado grew more and more outrageous. He had looted the Cuban treasury of millions, and to silence criticism his private gunmen beat, tortured, murdered, and generally terrorized people suspected of opposition to his rule. Desperate Cubans, pointing out that the Platt Amendment gave the United States the right to intervene in Cuba's domestic affairs, appealed to President Franklin D. Roosevelt to "do something."

Opposed to intervention in principle, FDR nevertheless sent warships to Cuban waters and ordered the U.S. ambassador in Havana to demand Machado's resignation and to arrange for new elections. Machado was bundled off into exile, and Carlos Manuel de Céspedes was elected president of a new provisional government. His term in office lasted just over twenty days, and during that time Roosevelt made it clear that he was opposed to the Platt Amendment and intended never to invoke it again.* And so, when Céspedes was driven from office by a little-known sergeant named Fulgencio Batista, the United States did nothing to prevent it.

A former cane-cutter, Batista simply walked into the army chief of staff's office, drew his pistol and dismissed him. He then appointed himself the new chief of staff with the rank of colonel. Extremely popular among the military rank and file, Batista fired hundreds of officers and replaced them with his own followers. With the backing of the army, Batista unquestionably was the boss, but he chose to operate as a behind-the-scenes strongman, making and breaking presidents as he wished. He was confident of his power, and so Batista permitted the elected congress, the newspapers, and the students to criticize the government and its policies. He gave encouragement to Cuba's labor unions and had their leaders placed in high government positions.

By 1939, Batista had gained the support of many liberal and left-wing groups, including the Communists. By now his hold was so secure that he was ready to experiment

---

*The United States signed a treaty in May 1934 releasing Cuba from the hobbles of the thirty-three-year-old Platt Amendment.

with democracy. At Batista's bidding, elections for a constituent assembly were held, and it wrote a constitution that was one of the most democratic in the hemisphere. Under the Constitution of 1940, all citizens, men and women, had the right to vote and form political parties. Presidential elections were to be held every four years. The constitution also stated that it was the duty of government to provide education, prevent unemployment, regulate working hours and conditions, and maintain programs of social insurance.

Batista stepped down as chief of staff in 1940 to run for president in the first election under the new constitution. By most accounts it was a fair election, and with the support of a wide range of political parties Batista won by a three-to-two margin over Dr. Ramón Grau San Martín. After a relatively uneventful term, during which Cuba prospered due to a boom in wartime trade with the United States, Batista did something that stunned many people. He stepped aside, allowed new elections to be held, and—having grown exceedingly rich at the expense of the Cuban people—retired to a sumptuous estate in Florida.

The next eight years were a disaster for Cuba's experiment with democracy. Grau San Martín succeeded Batista and he found it impossible to stamp out the corruption that Batista had allowed to flourish in the army, police, and civil service. Popular support for Grau San Martín crumbled when it became evident that he was following precedent by looting the Cuban treasury. In 1948, Carlos Prío Socarrás was elected president, but he proved ineffectual and soon his own honesty came into question. No one was surprised when it was discovered that he was building a $3 million house on his $25,000-a-year salary. With the government floundering and unrest growing, leaders of the business community and the army called on Batista to take power again. In March 1952, he ousted Prío Socarrás and sent him into exile. Batista thus put an end to a rare period of democracy that he himself had begun.

On his return to power, Batista found a different Cuba. Students at the University of Havana rioted frequently in behalf of left-wing, anti-American causes. They could point to the fact that Americans dominated the Cuban economy, owning over 90 percent of the telephone and electricity services, 50 percent of public transport and railways, and 40 percent of raw sugar production. The presence of well-to-do American tourists at Havana's plush hotels, casinos, and houses of prostitution added to anti-Yankee, anti-government feelings. Unfortunately for Batista, the sugar market took a sharp tumble, causing per capita income in the island to fall by 18 percent in one year. As unemployment rose and poverty intensified in the cities and countryside, left-wing unions called a series of anti-government strikes.

In the face of the unrest, Batista took a hard line. He curtailed freedom of speech and assembly. The army and police were used to terrorize opposition leaders, and courts martial and firing squads became commonplace. As rumors spread that Batista was adding to his already substantial fortune by taking protection money from the American crime syndicates that controlled Havana's gambling casinos, the atmosphere of corruption, brutality, and labor unrest became so intense that those Cuban business, professionals, and military men who had supported the strongman's return now began to turn against him.

FIDEL CASTRO'S REVOLUTION

Clearly, Fulgencio Batista had gone too far; his overthrow was only a matter of time, and Fidel Castro was only too willing to hasten the military dictator's downfall. Member of a well-to-do family and a dedicated Marxist-Leninist since his days as a student at Havana University, Castro launched his revolution in 1953 with the "26 July Manifesto" denouncing Batista, the wealthy Cubans, and foreign economic interests. This was followed by the ill-fated attempt to secure arms by attacking the Moncada army barracks in Santiago, a rash adventure in which most of Castro's young revolutionary band was mowed down by machine-gun fire. The survivors, including Fidel Castro and his brother Raúl, fled into the hills, but later the Castro brothers were taken prisoner and given long jail sentences. After they had served seventeen months, however, Batista pardoned them and set them free—a decision he would live to regret. Castro immediately left for Mexico to plan his next attempt against the Batista regime.

In December 1956, Castro landed with a band of eighty-two men on the southeast coast of Cuba, and once again they suffered heavy losses at the hands of Batista's troops. But this time, the Castro brothers and ten others escaped into the jungle-covered mountains of the Sierra Maestra. News of their survival filtered out, and soon dozens, then hundreds, of young Cubans found their way into the mountains to join them. Sympathizers in the United States, Mexico, and Venezuela smuggled arms, food, and medicine into the Sierra Maestra. Newspapers around the world, including influential papers in the United States, portrayed the Castro force as fighters for freedom and democracy.

Slowly, the rebels forged themselves into a guerrilla army, leaving their mountain lair to attack government outposts or to ambush government supply trucks loaded with food and ammunition. They cultivated good relations with the peasants, who gave them food and information about government troop movements. As their strength increased, Raúl Castro established another stronghold in the Sierra del Cristal in Oriente province. Batista's troops were unable to eradicate the revolutionary guerrillas, and the rebels began to attract the support of much of Cuba's unhappy middle class. These professionals and businessmen agreed with the guerrillas that the Batista regime was rotten and that the Yankees had too much influence. In pursuit of liberal, middle-class support, Castro masked his true political beliefs by saying that he would replace the dictatorship with a government elected according to the democratic 1940 constitution.

In March 1958, Cuban business leaders and landowners—by now totally fed up with Batista—asked the United States to halt arms sales to the government. Cubans of every class joined in the appeal, and the administration of President Dwight D. Eisenhower finally cut off the arms flow. As the influence of Castro's guerrillas spread, Cuban army officers began to panic. Top-ranking army officers fled into exile with whatever booty they could scramble together. Aware that his regime was collapsing around him, Batista was driven to the airport for a plane that would take him into exile in the Dominican Republic and later in Europe. The deposed tyrant fled with an estimated $200 million, all the while denouncing the Yankees for their failure to support his regime.

CASTRO TAKES POWER

Once in power in Havana, Castro and his revolutionaries moved decisively. They replaced senior government officials with people loyal to the revolution, and they purged the armed forces and police of Batista supporters. Amid cries of "al paredón" ("to the wall"), they lined up almost five hundred former Batista aides and officers and shot them without real trials. For the time being, Castro still needed the support of democratic opinion, and so liberal democrats were given a few non-influential places in the cabinet. One of them, Manuel Lleo Urrutia, was installed as a puppet president.

At the same time, Castro addressed Cuba's economy with revolutionary fervor—and innocence. Under the first Agrarian Reform Law, the state took over large cattle, sugar, and tobacco estates. Compensation for the land, in the form of government bonds, was promised, starting in four years. No compensation was promised for machinery and cattle. The seizure of privately owned land, much of which was parcelled out to landless families, continued throughout 1959 and 1960. By the end of that time, most of the land once owned by U.S. companies was in the hands of the Cuban state or Cuban peasants.

Castro and his followers believed that the true road to Cuba's economic salvation was that of rapid, government-managed industrialization. Using the Soviet Union as a model, the new rulers in Havana hoped to concentrate on mining, energy production, and heavy industry. But this required money and technical assistance, and so the young Marxist-Leninists in control of Cuba naturally turned to the bastion of Marxist-Leninist power, the Soviet Union. The Moscow government, eager to gain an ideological ally on America's doorstep, was pleased to oblige. With unusual swiftness, the Soviets made low-interest loans to the Castro government and entered into large-scale trade agreements with Cuba.

Once its ties with the Soviet Union were solidly established, the Castro government took a tough line with the United States. In 1960 Cuba cancelled leases held by U.S. companies to mine iron ore, sulphur, cobalt, and nickel. A short time later, the Cuban government seized U.S.-owned oil refineries and sugar mills. "We will take and take," said Castro, "until not even the nails of their shoes are left." When Castro refused to reply to American complaints that compensation offered for the seized U.S. property (about $1.5 billion worth) was inadequate, Congress cut off Cuban sugar imports and imposed an embargo on all shipments from the United States to Cuba, except for food and medicine.

In Cuba, many liberals who had supported Castro against Batista began to understand that he was establishing a Communist state closely allied with the Soviet Union.* In 1960, Castro forced Urrutia to resign as presi-

---

*On December 2, 1961, during a radio-TV broadcast, Castro proclaimed, "I am a Marxist-Leninist and will be one until the day I die." Castro went on to state that he had concealed his Communist views in order to court "bourgeois" support during his rise to power.

dent and ousted other liberals from the cabinet. Despite earlier promises to establish a democratic state, the Cuban government banned political opposition, outlawed free speech and an independent press, and threw thousands of political critics into prison. Middle-class Cubans, many of them professionals, managers, and skilled technicians, packed up and fled to the United States. In January 1961, after accusing the United States of plotting with his Cuban opponents, Castro demanded that the United States cut its sizable embassy staff in Havana to eleven within a week. President Eisenhower, whom Castro insulted as a "gangster" and a "senile White House golfer," had endured enough. With the support of Congress and the overwhelming majority of Americans, he severed diplomatic relations on January 4, 1961, a little over two weeks before president-elect John F. Kennedy inherited the prickly Cuban problem.

KENNEDY AND CUBA

Over the course of 1960, it had slowly dawned on the American public and on American politicians, Republican and Democrat alike, that Castro's government in Havana was not just an anti-Yankee irritant but the hemisphere's first firmly entrenched Communist regime. As such, it was dedicated to total state control over all facets of Cuba's economic, social and political life. It was aligned closely with the Soviet Union and the other Communist countries of eastern Europe. It openly advocated the export of its revolution to other countries in Latin America. Since this took place during the depths of the Cold War between the Communist world and the West, little wonder that many Americans believed that the overthrow of Castro's government would be a salutary thing for the United States, the Caribbean, and Latin America.

In an effort to topple the Castro government in Cuba, the Eisenhower administration had the U.S. Central Intelligence Agency recruit, arm, and train a group of exiled Cubans for an assault on the island. The operation, however, was all but doomed from the start. The tiny army of 1,500 anti-Castro Cubans was trained with obsolete American weapons and equipment in Guatemala. In addition, the "secret" preparations were common knowledge not only to Castro, who had spies among the Cuban exile group, but also to the American press.

When John F. Kennedy became president in January 1961, he inherited the invasion plan. Although he doubted its wisdom, the pressures to go ahead were strong, especially since he had promised during his campaign to do something about Communist Cuba and the hostility of Fidel Castro. But the new president insisted that under no circumstances would United States armed forces become directly involved. This meant that the invaders would be denied the air support they expected. As a result, when 2,000 Cuban exiles waded ashore at Bahía de Cochinos (the Bay of Pigs) on the southern coast of Cuba on April 17, 1961, they were quickly routed by Castro's heavily armed defenders. Within days, over a thousand survivors were rounded up and shipped off to Cuban prisons. The Bay of Pigs was a damaging blow to American prestige. To many, it also seemed to violate the spirit, if not the letter, of the United Nations Charter and that of the Organization of American States, both of which forbid unilateral interference in the internal affairs of fellow members.

But if the Bay of Pigs adventure was a fiasco for U.S. policy, the Kennedy administration gained considerable prestige for its handling of the Cuban missile crisis of 1962. This nerve-wracking episode began in late August, when high-flying U.S. reconnaissance planes photographed Soviet nuclear missiles being installed in Cuba by Russian technicians. At first Soviet Premier Nikita Khrushchev denied any knowledge of such activity, but new aerial photographs delivered to the White House on October 14 showed that Khrushchev had lied. Launching pads and missiles were indeed being placed in western Cuba, within easy striking distance of the United States and many Latin American countries. Khrushchev, operating through Castro, was making a bold attempt to alter the world balance of military power.

After a few days of debate within his administration, President Kennedy acted resolutely. There was no time for prolonged discussion in the United Nations, since the Soviet missiles would soon be operational. Instead, Kennedy urgently requested—and received—the unanimous support of the members of the Organization of American States for a U.S. plan to stop and search all Soviet ships bound for Cuba. He then demanded that the Soviet Union remove the missiles and ordered 150,000 U.S. troops to stand by for an invasion of Cuba, if that should become necessary. The world watched anxiously. If Soviet ships refused to stop and be searched for offensive weapons, American commanders were authorized to fire on them; if the Russians fired back, the confrontation might lead to a nuclear world war.

After a stressful week, Khrushchev backed away from the collision course. On October 28, 1962, he ordered Soviet ships bound for Cuba to turn back rather than to challenge the U.S. blockade. Following the exchange of a number of tense messages, Khrushchev agreed to pull the missiles out of Cuba, under verification by United Nations representatives. Kennedy agreed to lift the "quarantine" and not invade the island.

The Kennedy–Khrushchev agreement was never fully honored. The Soviets did crate up their missiles and ship them home with remarkable speed. But Fidel Castro, humiliated by the withdrawal caused by Kennedy's firmness, refused to permit on-site inspection by the United Nations. Given this, the United States apparently was released from its pledge not to invade Cuba. In the end, the missile crisis increased the prestige of the Kennedy administration and revealed to many in the Western Hemisphere that Fidel Castro had become a tool of the Soviet Union's global ambitions.

EXPORTING THE REVOLUTION

The mid-1960s saw Castro consolidate his regime and openly acknowledge its Communist nature. The one party permitted to exist was renamed the Communist party of Cuba. Fidel Castro was first secretary of the party, head of the Cuban government, and commander-in-chief of the armed forces. His brother Raúl Castro was defense minister, and only people of proven loyalty to Castro and the revolution remained in positions of power.

Despite massive amounts of aid from the Soviet Union, Cuba continued to endure severe economic problems throughout the 1960s and 1970s. A sharp decline in agricultural productivity led to serious food shortages, rationing, and a flourishing black market. Dropping its earlier emphasis on heavy industry, the Cuban government paid more attention to agriculture. In an attempt to improve efficiency, almost all small farms were organized into large collectives owned by the state and not by individual Cubans. As in the Soviet Union and other countries with collectivized agriculture, production was disappointing. The Cuban farm workers simply refused to work hard in fields that were not their own.

Severe problems at home, however, did not stop the Castro government from trying to export its revolutionary ideas to the rest of Latin America. The Cubans sent agents to Guatemala, Honduras, Costa Rica, Bolivia, Colombia, and Venezuela to support local Communist movements. They provided arms and money to anti-government guerrillas in the Dominican Republic and Haiti. Ché Guevara, Castro's close friend and ardent co-revolutionary, was assigned the task of carrying the revolution to South America. Guevara hoped to make the Andes the "Sierra Maestra of South America"; instead, he was captured in Bolivia, where he was organizing a Bolivian Army of Liberation. On October 9, 1967, Guevara was shot and killed by Bolivian soldiers.

The early 1970s saw an easing of tensions between the United States and the Soviet Union, and following the Soviet pattern, Cuba no longer talked openly of supporting international revolution. But in 1975, apparently at the bidding of Moscow, Castro sent thousands of troops to Angola to support the Communist side in the civil war that erupted when that African country gained its independence from Portugal. The Cuban intervention was of critical importance. The Communists won control of Angola, and as of 1984 some 25,000 to 35,000 Cuban troops remained in the country to protect the government from anti-Communist guerrillas. Castro also sent around 15,000 troops to Ethiopia in 1978 to help its Marxist-Leninist government beat back an invasion by neighboring Somalia.

In return for huge amounts of aid from the Soviet Union, whose political ideology Cuba shared, the Cuban armed forces had become an instrument of Soviet foreign policy. But in addition to exporting its military muscle, Cuba also sent technical missions to many parts of Africa and Latin America in the 1970s. The Cubans built schools, hospitals, and mass housing, but they also dabbled in local political affairs. Cuba's diplomatic mission was expelled from Jamaica after pro-Castro socialist Michael Manley lost the presidential election of 1980. And in 1983, its missions were ousted from Grenada, after the U.S.-led invasion, and from Suriname, whose own left-wing military government believed the Cubans were interfering in its domestic affairs.

In the early 1980s, Castro's Cuba gave strong support, including arms, supplies, and technical assistance, to the left-wing Sandinista regime in Nicaragua. Cuba was also accused of helping to arm and advise leftist rebels fighting to bring down the government of El Salvador. Castro denied the charge, but on January 2, 1984, in a speech marking the twenty-fifth anniversary of his rule in Cuba, he pledged to continue his aid to Marxist-Leninist revolutionaries around the world.

A QUARTER-CENTURY IN POWER

In his anniversary address, Castro claimed that Cuba, under his rule, had made great gains in providing health care and eliminating illiteracy. Most candid observers probably would accept that claim. Castro also stated that his government had eradicated prostitution, gambling, and drug trafficking in Cuba. The Communists had indeed eliminated much of this sordid activity, most people agreed, but the word "eradicated" was an exaggeration. In his speech, the Cuban dictator insisted that the country had made great economic gains under his leadership. That claim, critics noted, was totally without foundation. After twenty-five years of Castro's absolute rule, real economic growth was negligible. The country was deeply in debt to the Soviet Union and to western European bankers. Attempts to diversify the economy by encouraging small industry and tourism had failed dismally, since foreign investors did not feel comfortable sinking money into enterprises in Cuba. As a result, after a quarter-century under Castro's rule, Cuba remained largely a one-crop economy, based on sugar, and dependent on foreign largesse.

Whatever gains Communist Cuba may have made in the name of economic "equality," its failure in the realm of personal and political liberty has been monumental. Like Cuban dictators of the past, Castro permitted no political liberties and operated a wide network of informers who reported the slightest anti-government activity. In 1980, the government began a new crackdown on dissidents. The oppressive political atmosphere, plus a severe economic crisis, caused 125,000 more Cubans to flee to the United States in an enormous "sea-lift." The Havana government wisely let the unhappy Cubans depart, opening the port of Mariel for ships to load them aboard and set sail for Florida. In this latest of Castro's open-exit policies, Cuba rid itself of many discontented urban workers. Castro also emptied some of his prison cells and included an unknown number of common criminals in the exodus to the United States; some were discovered and detained but many others melted into the growing Cuban-American community. The 1980 sea-lift brought the number of refugees from Castro's Cuba to at least one million.

Not so fortunate were Cuba's prisoners of conscience. As of early 1984, many thousands of them remained in prison, sometimes under vile conditions, for nothing more than opposing the Communist state. Among these prisoners were not only people convicted of violent acts of rebellion but also peasants who resisted collective farming, youths who resisted military service in Angola, workers who tried to organize free unions, people who tried to leave the country without permission, and former revolutionaries who opposed Communism and expressed "counterrevolutionary" views. According to prisoners who gained release, the harshest treatment in Castro's jails was accorded to the more than 200 religious prisoners who refuse to accept Marxist indoctrination.

Thus, Cuba in the early 1980s was a troubled but militarily strong Caribbean country. Despite Cuba's many problems, including an almost total dependence on Soviet aid for survival, most of its people apparently remained loyal to the Castro regime. The country's influence in the Caribbean region was significant but far from dominant. Twenty-five years after Fidel Castro came to power, Cuba remained the only Communist state in the Caribbean—an object of intense interest and deep suspicion to most other countries in the region.

CHAPTER
■6■
CHALLENGE
AND
RESPONSE

Fidel Castro, with the backing of the Soviet Union, showed that he could thumb his nose at the United States—the Yankee colossus—and survive. As a result, the Castro regime in Cuba inspired revolutionaries throughout the Caribbean and Latin America during the 1960s, 1970s, and early 1980s. Fearful of a proliferation of left-wing, pro-Soviet countries on its southern doorstep, the United States responded to the increasing unrest in a number of ways, shifting between Theodore Roosevelt's policy of intervention and Franklin Roosevelt's policy of the Good Neighbor.

THE ALLIANCE FOR PROGRESS

In the late 1950s, talk was plentiful in Washington about the need for a Marshall Plan for Latin America, like the program financed by the United States to assist the recovery of western Europe after World War II. The rise of Castro and other revolutionary movements made it clear that heroic measures would have to be taken to improve the conditions of life in the Caribbean and the rest of Latin America if further Communist triumphs were to be avoided. In 1960, the Eisenhower administration promised to contribute $500 million to the Inter-American Social Development Fund, the money to finance economic and social improvements in Latin America. The U.S. proposal, which seemed to be a response to Fidel Castro's boat-rocking in the Caribbean, led many cynical Latinos to call the Eisenhower proposal the "Fidel Castro Plan."

Soon after taking office in 1961, President John F. Kennedy radically increased the amount of Latin American aid Eisenhower had offered. Kennedy proposed a new ten-year, $20-billion program, most of it to be paid for by the United States, for social and economic development in the Caribbean, Central America, and South America. The program was called the Alliance for Progress (*Alianza para Progreso*), suggesting a partnership of nations. After the Bay of Pigs disaster, Kennedy redoubled his efforts to get the Alliance under way. In May 1961, Congress appropriated the first $500 million. The next significant step came in August, when the Inter-American Economic and Social Council met in Punta del Este, Uruguay, and subscribed to a charter for the Alliance for Progress that pledged to "secure a better life under freedom and democracy for present and future generations." The Alliance, stated the Charter, aimed to speed social and economic development, improve housing, education, and health care, and create fairer societies by assuring a just distribution of land and a better life for the working man.

The rhetoric may have been inflated, but simply stated, the Alliance for Progress was meant to encourage America's southern neighbors to help themselves. The United States indeed would provide most of the money, but that was not supposed to be just a handout from Uncle Sam's bulging moneybags. As their part of the Alliance, the various hemispheric countries were to take concrete steps to eradicate the appalling poverty and social conditions which spawned unrest and revolution.

Unfortunately, the Alliance did not come close to achieving its goals, for a number of reasons. For one thing, the U.S. Congress required that 60 percent of the funds contributed by the United States be spent on the purchase of goods from American companies. This forced Caribbean and Latin American countries to buy U.S.-made machinery, for example, when it was available more cheaply in Japan or Europe. In addition, Congress specified that no U.S. funds could be spent on projects that might compete with private enterprise. The major blame, however, lay with the countries of the Caribbean and Latin America, which proved incapable of living up to their part of the bargain as envisaged by the Alliance. Radicals on the left saw it as an attempt to apply an economic Band-Aid to serious and deep deficiencies in the social system. On the political right, the Alliance was viewed as anti-capitalist, since it would have encouraged many public projects; governments were either unwilling or afraid to make reforms that would cause distress to the wealthier classes. "The Alliance was demanding social change of us faster than we could safely produce it," commented a Caribbean businessman. "It required a commitment we couldn't give."

Little could be accomplished as long as the Alliance had to work through governments unable to support the needed economic and social change. And so, in the end, the Alliance faded quietly from sight, having done little to bring significant change to the Caribbean or Latin America as a whole. The American dollars all too often found their way into the pockets of the wealthy, and from there into Swiss bank accounts. In the Caribbean, the Alliance did make a few solid achievements. Guyana used its money to build new roads, construct an airport, and improve its water supplies. Haiti was helped to reclaim land for farming and to build its tourist industry. But if the Alliance for

Progress was perhaps better than nothing, it remained on balance an expensive failure.

LBJ INVADES THE DOMINICAN REPUBLIC

In addition to ambitious economic and social schemes such as the Alliance for Progress, American presidents also resorted on occasion to the old policy of direct U.S. military intervention in the Caribbean. The Dominican Republic is a case in point, and here we must backtrack for some historical perspective.

When the U.S. Marines were pulled out of the Dominican Republic in 1924 by President Calvin Coolidge, they left behind an elected government and a well-armed local police force. But in 1930, when President Horacio Vásquez tried to retain power in a rigged election, he was thrown out of office by the police force. The leader of the police was Rafael Trujillo Molina, and once in power he made full use of his former colleagues to build a personal dictatorship that would dominate the Dominican Republic for more than three decades.

Trujillo ran an efficient dictatorship in which industry and agriculture performed well by Caribbean standards of the time. It also was one of the most brutal governments ever to afflict the region, using torture and murder to silence any opposition that dared to raise its head. And as the years went by, Trujillo became richer and richer at the expense of the Dominican people. Along with members of his family and selected associates, the dictator owned or controlled 75 percent of the economic activity in the country. In the late 1950s, opposition to the aging Trujillo began to appear and mount in intensity. Finally, the United States concluded that Trujillo was an embarrassment to its policy in the region. U.S. aid to the Dominican Republic was cut off, a signal to anti-Trujillo Dominicans that Washington would not oppose a change. In May 1961, the change was made. Possibly with the help of the U.S. Central Intelligence Agency, unknown assassins riddled the strongman with bullets and put an end to his rule.

In December 1962, an honest election was held and Juan Bosch, a moderate socialist, was elected president. With the encouragement of the Kennedy administration, Bosch introduced a number of economic and social reforms. Among other things, his government confiscated millions of acres of land owned by the Trujillo family and distributed them to 70,000 landless families. The confiscations alarmed many in the business community, in the police force, and in the military, who feared that the wealth they amassed under Trujillo would be threatened by Bosch's reforms. In September 1963, the police arrested Bosch and sent him into exile. The elected congress was dismissed and a military junta headed by General Elias Wessin y Wessin was established.

Dissatisfaction with the military regime was widespread, and on April 24, 1965 pro-Bosch rebel army units seized control of two army posts and the main radio station in the capital of Santo Domingo. The fighting rapidly became so furious that thousands of Dominicans lost their lives, leading the American ambassador to urge President Lyndon B. Johnson to intervene for the protection of the hundreds of U.S. citizens in the country. Moreover, the embassy warned the president, a victory by the rebels—who included a few known Communists in their ranks—could lead to a Castro-style regime hostile to the United States. Unwilling to risk another Cuba in the Caribbean, Johnson ordered nearly 25,000 marines to land in the Dominican Republic and restore order.

The marines did restore order by keeping the contending sides from each other's throat, but Johnson's iron-fisted intervention—the first in many decades—violated solemn U.S. treaty commitments to the Organization of American States and the United Nations. In many parts of the hemisphere, outraged people denounced the breaking of the near-sacred principle of nonintervention and demanded "Yankee, Go Home!" Not since Franklin Roosevelt disavowed intervention in 1933 had American armed forces desecrated Caribbean shores. In doing so, President Johnson demonstrated that the United States would still take unilateral action in the Caribbean if it perceived its own interests to be threatened. Teddy Roosevelt's corollary to the Monroe Doctrine was not dead after all.

When he ordered the marines into the Dominican Republic, Johnson also called for a special session of the Organization of American States. It quickly convened, and the United States asked that the hemispheric body approve the creation of an Inter-American Peace Force to keep order in the Dominican Republic until a new government could be elected. The OAS authorized the force by a vote of 14 to 5, and, in the weeks that followed, troops from Nicaragua, Honduras, Paraguay, Costa Rica, and Brazil were sent to the Dominican Republic under the command of a Brazilian general.

The American marines withdrew, but the U.S. Ambassador to the OAS, Ellsworth Bunker, remained behind to make certain that General Wessin y Wessin and his accomplices were removed from power and sent out of the country to unimportant posts. With the blessing of the OAS, the Dominican Republic held new elections in June 1966. The two rivals for the presidency were Juan Bosch, who had drifted into a more militant left-wing stance, and a moderate right-winger named Joaquín Balaguer. The pro-American Balaguer, who emphasized peace and order as well as land reform, won by a surprisingly large margin. The Dominicans had voted for gradual, orderly progress over wrenching social change.

After 1966, the Dominican Republic enjoyed a series of peaceful and honest elections. Balaguer, backed by his Reformist party, won again in 1970 and 1974. But in 1978, the aging conservative lost the election to Antonio Guz-

mán Fernández, leader of the middle-of-the-road Dominican Revolutionary party. For the first time in the country's
134-year history, power was peacefully transferred to the
opposition after an election. In 1982, when Guzmán
decided not to run for another term, and then unaccount-
ably committed suicide, he was succeeded by Jorge Blan-
co, also of the Dominican Revolutionary party.

THE CUBAN HAND

During the 1970s, Castro's Cuba played a significant role
in at least three Caribbean countries: Jamaica, Grenada,
and Suriname. None in any way became a satellite of
Cuba, but the growth of Havana's influence in the three
became a source of concern in the United States and in
the democratic countries of the Caribbean. The American
response was different in each instance, varying from a
worried hands-off policy in the case of Jamaica to outright
military intervention in Grenada and anti-government plotting in Suriname.

Jamaica. ▪ After independence in 1962, Jamaica retained
a two-party system, with the People's National party (PNP)
and the Jamaica Labor party (JLP) bidding for the support
of the electorate. The PNP, headed first by Norman Manley
and in recent years by his son Michael Manley, was a democratic socialist party that favored a large amount of state
ownership of industry and services as well as centralized
government planning. The JLP, founded by Alexander
Bustamante and later headed by Edward Seaga, was a
more pragmatic party, eager to make solid gains for Jamaica's working people but basically through a program
emphasizing private enterprise and close ties to the United States.

Through most of the 1970s, the freely-elected Jamaican government was run by Michael Manley and the PNP.
This period, however, was characterized by racial vio-

lence, attempts by the government to "socialize" the economy, and a disastrous decline in economic performance. It was also marked by a strong growth of Cuban influence on the island that disturbed many Jamaicans and the U.S. government. In 1974 Jamaica established diplomatic ties with Castro's Cuba for the first time, and in 1974 Castro made a state visit to the island and was warmly received by Prime Minister Manley. Shortly after, Manley brought in thousands of Cuban technicians and teachers to conduct building, education, and agricultural programs. Soon Cubans were seen in every part of the island. A large portrait of Fidel Castro hung on the wall of Manley's office.

Administrations in Washington and governments in the Caribbean kept a close watch on Manley's relations with Cuba. But the Jamaican prime minister did not tamper with the democratic processes in his country, and so the judgment on his policies was left to the voters of Jamaica. By 1980, apparently they had had enough of Manley, the PNP, the poor economy, and the Cubans. In November, Seaga's JLP won a landslide victory, gaining 52 parliamentary seats to 9 for Manley's PNP. Once in office, Seaga changed Jamaica's course, emphasizing the role of private capital in economic development, renegotiating the country's foreign debt with the international banking community, and wooing American tourists and their dollars. Seaga also stressed close ties with the United States and expressed deep distrust of Cuba and its intentions in the Caribbean. The Cuban technicians and teachers were sent home.

In 1983, Seaga—still popular despite Jamaica's uphill struggle for economic prosperity—unexpectedly called a parliamentary election. Polls showed that Manley's PNP, weak, disorganized, and lacking in funds, would lose badly once again, and unwilling to risk defeat, Manley and his party boycotted the elections held on December 15. As a result, Seaga's JLP won all 60 seats in parliament. Manley's tactics had clouded an election that he had little change of winning.

Grenada ▪ In March 1979, Sir Eric Gairy, the erratic and despotic leader who became prime minister of Grenada upon independence in 1974, was ousted in a coup. The leader of the revolt was British-educated lawyer Maurice Bishop, and soon he and his Marxist New Jewel Movement were running the island country with an iron hand. The parliamentary system of government inherited from the British was dismantled, political opposition was outlawed, and critics among the Grenadan population were jailed. Sir Paul Scoon, the governor general who—as in all countries which choose membership in the British Commonwealth— was the representative of the British crown, was placed under house arrest.

Bishop, a charismatic leader and an admirer of Fidel Castro, invited the Cubans in for the usual reasons such as building roads and medical clinics and giving athletic instruction. Soon, however, the island was being visited by an extraordinary number of representatives from Communist bloc nations—not only Cubans but Russians, East Germans, and North Koreans. One of their chief projects was the construction of a 10,000-foot (3,048-m)-long airport runway at Port Salines, a runway that could accommodate long-range Soviet bombers and advanced jet aircraft. Grenada's neighbors in the Caribbean were understandably nervous about the Communist military buildup on the island.

The full extent of this buildup on Grenada was not known outside the island. Nor did outsiders know about the deadly political infighting that was going on within Bishop's ruling New Jewel Movement. The struggle involved Bishop on one side and his senior deputy, Bernard Coard on the other. Coard and his followers, strong supporters of the Soviet Union, did not think that Bishop was sufficiently militant in his pursuit of true Marxist-Leninism. When Bishop rejected their demands that he share power with them, he was placed under house arrest on October 13, 1983, by troops under the direction of General Hudson Austin, an ally of Coard.

On October 19, an angry crowd of Bishop's supporters released him from house arrest, only to be confronted by General Austin's troops. What happened next is open to dispute. Coard and Austin later maintained that Bishop and a number of his supporters died when Bishop tried to seize the Fort Rupert army barracks and shooting broke out. On the other hand, witnesses said that Bishop and his colleagues surrendered to the soldiers and that they later were executed. Whatever the truth about Bishop's fate, Bernard Coard and General Austin seized control of Grenada.

The killing of Bishop and his supporters, plus the general chaos that ensued on the island, intensified the fears of Grenada's eastern Caribbean neighbors. On October 23, leaders of the Organization of Eastern Caribbean States called upon the United States to intervene. Emerging from house arrest, Sir Paul Scoon—a representative of whatever legality still remained on Grenada—joined in the appeal for American intervention.

The Reagan administration saw an opportune moment to remove Grenada from the pro-Castro camp. Moreover, the need for forceful action was heightened by the presence on Grenada of about 1,000 Americans, most of them students at St. George's University School of Medicine. The Americans may or may not have been in any danger, but Coard and Austin were perceived as extremist figures capable of life-threatening action. On October 25, President Reagan acted. Over four thousand American troops were landed, some by sea, others by air. With the Americans were about 300 troops from eastern Caribbean countries. Most of the resistance came from the Cubans on the island, but in a few days U.S. forces were in firm control of Grenada.

In the days that followed, the American residents on the island were flown back to the United States. The U.S. troops, whose strength had been increased to 7,000 men, mopped up lingering resistance, rounded up Communist-bloc advisors on the island and sent them home, and supported Governor General Scoon in his efforts to restore order and a semblance of legitimate government. Bernard Coard and General Austin were taken into custody, presumably for eventual trial for the murder of Maurice Bishop and others.

Exploring the island, American troops uncovered a huge supply of Soviet-bloc arms, far more than tiny Grenada could possibly have needed for its own defense. In addition, the Americans found copies of secret pacts between Grenada and Cuba, the Soviet Union, and North Korea, calling for the delivery of $37 million worth of additional arms and the permanent basing of Cuban military advisors on the island. The tremendous arms buildup, the military agreements and the feverish work on the Port Salines runway led to the inescapable conclusion that Cuba and the Soviet Union had been planning to make Grenada into a base for training regional revolutionaries or a depot for the transshipment of arms to Central and South America.

The legality of the American intervention in Grenada was the subject of great controversy, in the United States and abroad. The action was condemned by the United Nations and criticized by U.S. allies in Europe. But as a political move, there was little doubt that the Grenada invasion added up to a stinging rebuff to Cuban and Soviet ambitions in the Caribbean. This was not achieved without a price. Official statistics stated that eighteen American soldiers were killed and 115 wounded in action; forty-five Grenadans and twenty-four Cubans were also killed.

In December, all American combat forces were withdrawn from Grenada. Left behind was a "residual element" of 300 U.S. troops, whose mission was to help the

Caribbean force, by then numbering 500, maintain order and train Grenadan police. As a first step toward the restoration of a legitimate civilian government, Governor General Scoon appointed a nine-member "advisory council" to reassemble a governmental structure and a civil service, both almost totally dismantled during Bishop's years of one-man rule. In January 1984, Scoon chose a supervisor of elections to get electoral machinery in place within a year. But the political life of the island-country was in such disarray that it would not be easy to establish democratic processes and a government able to stand on its own feet.

Suriname ▪ When Suriname gained its independence from the Netherlands in 1975, this potentially rich country on the northern coast of South America had a Western-style parliamentary democracy. But in 1980 a group of disgruntled left-wing officers led by Lt. Colonel Desi Bouterse overthrew the elected government and installed a military dictatorship. Bouterse, a friend of Grenada's Maurice Bishop and an admirer of Fidel Castro, promptly asked the Cuban government to send him military aid and advisors.

Blossoming relations with Cuba brought Suriname a flood of delegations, projects, and promises. The Cuban ambassador became the toast of the capital of Paramaribo. In short order, he was involved in almost every aspect of government business. It was apparent that the democratic countries of the Caribbean had to worry about another pro-Cuban outpost in their midst.

In December 1982, Bouterse announced that a coup sponsored by the U.S. Central Intelligence Agency had been foiled. In the wake of the alleged plot, at least fifteen prominent critics of the military regime—including union leaders and journalists—were rounded up and executed. Incensed by the brutality, the Netherlands and the United

■ 80 ■

States suspended aid to Suriname. Bouterse, however, may have had grounds for suspicion about the CIA. In May 1983, it was revealed in Washington that there had indeed been a plan to overthrow Bouterse but that it was dropped because of objections by congressional committees which provide legislative review of American intelligence operations. In November 1983, Bouterse again claimed to have put down a coup attempt, this time by mercenaries recruited by Surinamese exiles living in the Netherlands.

Coups were not Colonel Bouterse's only cause of concern. In late 1983, strikes erupted in Suriname's critically important bauxite industry. In January 1984, the strikes spread to commercial banks and electric power companies. For periods of time, electric power was totally cut off in Paramaribo, and it appeared that the real objective of the strikers was to bring down the military regime of Desi Bouterse.

Fearful that he had made too many powerful enemies, Bouterse reassessed his position in late 1983. Despite promises to nationalize American- and Dutch-owned bauxite facilities, he moved with the utmost caution. He also promised to form a "democratic revolutionary" government that would permit civilian participation in decision making. But Bouterse's biggest surprise was his sharp reversal on the Cubans. On October 25, the same day as the U.S.-led invasion of Grenada, Bouterse abruptly expelled eighty Cuban advisors and twenty-five Cuban embassy personnel, including the ambassador.

The colonel's motives in ousting the Cubans were far from clear. It was known that he was disturbed by Bishop's murder and may have suspected a Cuban role in that episode. He and his closest aides also had come to resent the growing Cuban interference in Suriname's internal policy debates. Bouterse, moreover, viewed Cuban contacts with lower-level Surinamese officials as an attempt to undercut his authority. In addition to these reasons, the colonel may have thought that he could placate his many enemies—including the United States—by kicking out the Cubans. Whatever Bouterse's motives might have been, the ouster of the Cubans was another serious setback for Castro in the Caribbean.

THE CARIBBEAN
BASIN INITIATIVE

In a speech before the Organization of American States on February 24, 1982, President Reagan warned of the danger that "new Cubas will arise from the ruins of today's conflicts." To help prevent a region full of Cubas, the president then unveiled his Caribbean Basin Initiative for the economic recovery of the Caribbean states and the circum-Caribbean countries of Honduras, Guatemala, and El Salvador. Like the Alliance for Progress before it, the new program emphasized that economic progress in the region would not only benefit the people but also render them less vulnerable to revolutionary appeals.

As originally proposed by the president, the CBI was to have three "legs": aid, investment, and trade. The overall objective was to generate badly needed foreign exchange, create new jobs, and raise production levels in the countries of the region. The initiative was to be carried out in cooperation with Canada, Venezuela, Colombia, and Mexico, all of which had similar programs of their own.

Specifically, the American program had the following aims: to (1) provide a "quick fix" of $350 million in supplementary economic aid, in addition to the $474.6 million already budgeted, for fiscal year 1982, (2) create an investment tax credit of 10 percent for American businesses investing in the Caribbean basin, and (3) establish duty-free access to the U.S. market for Caribbean Basin exports for a period of twelve years. The latter point, the so-called Free Trade Area, was regarded as the centerpiece of the initiative.

Congress quickly passed legislation granting the supplementary aid, but it deleted from the program the 10 percent tax incentive for Americans wishing to invest in the Caribbean. The proposal for duty-free access for Caribbean Basin exports was accepted by Congress, but only after it exempted textiles and apparel under pressure from U.S. unions. The duty-free access to the huge American market went into effect in January 1984, and the Reagan administration and Caribbean leaders hoped that it would provide the stimulus that all the economies of the region needed so badly. It would take a few years, however, to judge the success or failure of the Caribbean Basin Initiative.

The middle and later years of the 1980s undoubtedly will see new challenges made by Castro's Cuba and other revolutionary forces in the Caribbean. How the United States, the democratic governments of the region, and the people of the Caribbean respond to those challenges will be of critical importance to the hemisphere and, it is not too much to say, to the world.

CHAPTER
■7■
WHY CARE ABOUT THE CARIBBEAN?

America's involvement in the Caribbean is no longer a matter of choice but of necessity. Geography and history have seen to that. Even the most distant of Caribbean countries is closer to Washington, D.C., than is San Francisco. With justification, the Caribbean has been called our "third border" or "America's doorstep." Thus, events of any significance in the region are likely to affect the United States in one way or another. American interests in the Caribbean traditionally have been strategic, political, and economic. In the latter part of the 20th century, however, the American interest in the Caribbean increasingly took on a human dimension, as millions of people of the area migrated to the United States in search of economic betterment or personal freedom.

STRATEGIC CONCERNS

Since the early years of the American republic, the Caribbean has been of vital strategic concern. In the 19th century, administrations in Washington feared that one or more of the European powers might use their colonies in the region to threaten U.S. commerce or even mount an attack on the United States. In the 20th century, the importance of the Panama Canal to American military movements and commercial operations heightened the strategic importance of the Caribbean. Hoping to disrupt shipping through the canal, German submarines sank many ships in Caribbean waters during World War II. But in the latter part of the 20th century, the strategic threat to the United States was posed by the alliance of Communist Cuba with America's chief adversary, the Soviet Union. Just how dangerous this alliance could become was demonstrated by the Cuban missile crisis in 1962, when the world trembled on the edge of nuclear war.

Cuba's geographic position makes it of particular concern to the United States. Just 90 miles (145 km) off the coast of Florida, Cuba dominates the only two sea lanes in and out of the Gulf of Mexico. Moreover, aside from the United States, Cuba is by far the strongest military power in an area where many countries do not have or even want an army. Had Cuba been able to base its Soviet MIG jets on the airfield under construction in Grenada, its ability to menace the eastern Caribbean and northern South America would have been enhanced significantly. If Cuba should ever try to station Soviet combat forces on the island or allow the establishment of a Soviet naval base, it would be seen as a direct challenge to the United States.

It is not only the threat of direct attack that makes the Caribbean so strategically vital to the United States. Through the Caribbean moves much of the international shipping of the United States, western Europe, Japan, mainland Latin America, and the Caribbean countries themselves. Cargoes include such important items as petroleum from the Middle East as well as from Venezuela, Mexico, and the Caribbean. Nearly half of U.S. crude oil imports, and nearly half of all U.S. exports and imports, pass through these Caribbean sea lanes. A threat to them would be considered an act of aggression, not only by the United States but by a number of Latin American countries.

The Caribbean also produces raw materials of vital importance to the United States. Chief among them is bauxite mined in Jamaica, Suriname, and Guyana. Bauxite is important because one of its derivatives, alumina, is necessary for the manufacture of aluminum. Since the United States imports 90 percent of its bauxite, half of which comes from the Caribbean, this trade alone gives the Caribbean considerable strategic importance in the American economy. In addition, about 8 percent of U.S. requirements for primary nickel are imported from the Dominican Republic.

FELLOW DEMOCRACIES

In the early years of the 20th century, an American politician, noting the procession of dictatorial governments in the Caribbean, remarked that "bananas and democracy do not grow in the same climate." Regrettably, that comment has proven all too applicable to some parts of the world. But fortunately it does not apply to most of the Caribbean. An overwhelming number of the countries of the region have democratically elected governments and it is unlikely that this pattern will change radically in the near future. And where political democracy does not exist in the Caribbean, the United States hopes to encourage its growth.

Why? For both idealistic and practical reasons. If Americans believe in the value of democracy in the United States, they should wish to see it flourish in every part of the world, and particularly among our Caribbean neighbors. The United States, still regarded by billions of people around the world as the leading advocate and chief defender of democracy, cannot succumb to the "bananas and democracy" argument that the system may work for us but is not suitable for developing countries of the Third World.

It is also in the self-interest of the United States to support democratic government in the Caribbean and elsewhere. Democratic institutions, modern history will attest, provide the best framework for stable social and economic development. They offer channels for the redress of grievances. Democracy allows differences to be resolved through compromise before dangerous political pressures build and violence follows. Governments which do not heed the wishes of their people through free elections, free press, and free speech are far more likely to be tyrannical, inefficient, and a threat to peace.

THE ECONOMIC TIE

The American economic interest in the Caribbean is of two kinds. The first is obvious: it is a place for U.S. trade and investment. The second level of American economic concern with the region is more complex. It is the "enlightened self-interest" that understands that the United States will benefit if the people of the Caribbean overcome their economic problems and increase the well-being of their growing populations.

The region's share in American trade and investment, while not large by world standards, is nevertheless significant. In 1983, Caribbean exports to the United States were valued at $9 billion—more than seven times the figure for 1970. Expenditures by American tourists in the Caribbean for local goods and services came to at least another $1 billion. American exports to the Caribbean added up to a sizable $5.8 billion. In 1983, the Caribbean accounted for 3 percent of all U.S. exports and 3.5 percent of U.S. imports—the great bulk of the latter being petroleum, with bauxite, alumina, sugar, nickel, fruits, and vegetables making up the rest. In 1981, direct United States investment in the Caribbean (excluding Puerto Rico) was $10.1 billion, or 4 percent of all our direct foreign investment that year. Again, by world standards these figures are not high, but the American investment remains extremely important for the small Caribbean economies.

Of enormous concern to the United States was the pervasive economic crisis that gripped the Caribbean in the late 1970s and early 1980s. One cause of this was the decline in world prices for Caribbean exports such as bauxite, sugar, and coffee; another major cause was the steep rise in the price of oil which the island nations imported, and the rising interest rates on money borrowed overseas. This combination of economic factors dealt the region a severe setback. After years of steady growth in economic performance (as measured by gross national product—the total value of goods and services produced in a given period), some countries experienced years of zero growth or less. Unemployment soared, as did balance-of-payments difficulties and foreign debts. Under these economic circumstances, it was extraordinary that political unrest was kept to a minimum.

There was little question that the countries of the Caribbean needed additional outside financial assistance. Recognizing that fact, in 1977 the United States and the World Bank brought together a consortium of thirty-one aid-giving and aid-receiving countries to form the Caribbean Group for Co-operation in Economic Development. This organization, which coordinates foreign economic aid to all countries in the Caribbean except Cuba, places an emphasis on development projects requiring regional cooperation. In addition to financial assistance, the Caribbean countries badly needed expanding markets for their exports, within the Caribbean, in Europe, and especially in the United States. A significant increase in Caribbean exports to the United States could give a tremendous lift to the Caribbean economies. This is one of the objectives of President Reagan's Caribbean Basin Initiative; its success or failure will be judged in the mid- and late 1980s.

Within the Caribbean itself, important efforts were afoot—particularly among the English-speaking countries—to strengthen regional economic cooperation. The first step was to break down some of the barriers impeding trade among the Caribbean countries. In the pre-independence days of 1961, Guyana, Barbados, and Antigua took the first step, permitting goods to be imported from one territory to the other without paying customs duties. The results were so encouraging that the representatives of thirteen English-speaking Caribbean states and territories met in Guyana in 1968 and agreed to set up a Caribbean Free Trade Area. CARIFTA, as it was called, eliminated trade barriers such as customs duties on some agricultural products and many manufactures. As a result, trade among the members of CARIFTA grew at a brisk pace. For instance, beds, stoves, chemicals, garments, and medical supplies from Jamaica began to turn up in shops in Trinidad. In Jamaica, shoppers were able to compare Trinidadian matches, refrigerators, and processed foods with their own local products or foreign imports.

CARIFTA's success led to another step toward fuller regional cooperation in 1973, when its members replaced it with the Caribbean Common Market, or CARICOM. The new organization continued to encourage the growth of free trade among its members, but it also pledged to work toward a full-fledged customs union with a common tariff on imports from outside the market area. The adherence to a common tariff wall for products from outside the region, it was hoped, would encourage members to buy from each other. The common external tariff was not expected to be in place until the mid-1980s.

As a matter of self-interest, the United States supported these and other steps toward Caribbean regional economic integration. A widely shared view in Washington, among Republicans and Democrats alike, was that many of the smaller Caribbean states would find it difficult to survive as democracies unless they became part of a larger grouping with healthier economic prospects.

THE HUMAN DIMENSIONS

For centuries, the Caribbean has been a region of migrants. In need of a large supply of cheap labor for the sugar plantation, the colonists brought in millions of slaves from Africa and indentured servants from Asia. Migration in the late 19th and early 20th centuries had a different pattern. It was chiefly the movement of millions of individuals from place to place within the region in search of jobs, higher pay, or better living conditions. But in the middle decades of the 20th century, poor economic conditions, political turmoil, and a rapidly expanding population created a vast Caribbean diaspora, this time to the industrialized countries of western Europe and especially to the United States.

Immigrants from the islands of the British Caribbean were the first to arrive in the United States in significant numbers, in the second and third decades of the century. Their community grew substantially during World War II, as war industries clamored for workers, and many more came in the 1950s, 1960s, and 1970s, legally or otherwise. In 1980, conservative estimates were that 50,000 Barbadians, 150,000 Trinidadians, and half a million Jamaicans, plus lesser numbers from the smaller British Caribbean states, had settled in the United States. Most of them lived in the New York City area or in other large cities of the northeast.

Spanish-speaking Caribbean peoples did not begin to flood into the United States until after World War II. As American citizens, Puerto Ricans were free to come and go as they chose, and by 1980 the Puerto Rican population in the United States exceeded 2 million, or about 40 percent of all the Puerto Ricans in the world. Migration to the United States from the Dominican Republic did not begin until the 1960s, when economic troubles and political violence touched off a sizable exodus. In a period of fifteen years, about 400,000 Dominicans—8 percent of the country's entire population—moved to the United States. One of the largest, and certainly the most dramatic of all the Caribbean migrations, was the flight of nearly a million Cubans to the United States in the years since the Cuban revolution.

French-speaking Haitians began to arrive in the United States in the 1950s, when poor economic conditions and a harsh dictatorship forced many of the wealthier class to flee. In the 1960s and 1970s, middle-class and urban working-class Haitians reached the United States, legally and illegally, and in the mid-1970s it was estimated that over 300,000 Haitians lived in the New York City area alone. In the late 1970s, thousands of Haitian "boat people," who had risked their lives aboard flimsy craft in heavy seas, sailed into American waters. They were chiefly poor rural workers, and the U.S. government decided that these Haitians were not political refugees but people seeking economic betterment and, therefore, were not eligible for political sanctuary. Some were turned away from American shores, others were placed in camps until their cases could be decided. A small number disappeared illegally into the Haitian community in the United States.

For the Caribbean countries, the huge outward migration was a mixed blessing. It relieved unemployment problems at home and served as an escape valve for political discontent. It was a source of hard currency, since many of the Caribbean islanders living and working in the United States sent dollars to family members back home. But the migration to the north also created something of a "brain drain" in the Caribbean. Many of the people who left were highly educated, highly skilled professionals and intellectuals, who might have played leading roles in bringing progress to their own countries.

The great Caribbean migration, which continued in the mid-1980s, once again demonstrated how closely tied the United States is to the region to its southeast. How well the United States succeeds in digesting this wave of migration will become clearer as the century progresses. The hope was that the Caribbeans, like earlier immigrants, would become a stable community, taking their place among the many elements that make up America's diverse society. It may be a slow process, but in the end the United States and the Caribbean world inevitably will be bound together more firmly than ever before.

CHAPTER ■8■ THE ROAD AHEAD

Looking into the future is always a dangerous thing, and the future of the Caribbean is no exception. But let us start with some "best and worst" cases.

The worst case would be a Caribbean unable to cope with its deepening economic problems, ripped apart by political dissension and violence, incapable of sustained humane, democratic forms of government. Under these conditions, Marxism-Leninism could spread across the region, prompting new American interventions, either to prop up democracy or to protect U.S. interests. This action would doubtless lead to international protests about "Yankee interventionism" and possibly to military conflict with Cuba and the Soviet Union.

The best case would be a Caribbean which, with the aid of the United States, Canada, Venezuela, Colombia, Mexico and other hemispheric democracies, is able to overcome its economic miseries and significantly improve the lot of the masses of its people. In this scenario, the countries of the Caribbean would make substantial progress toward regional cooperation, through CARICOM and other organizations, thereby strengthening the foundation for stable, democratic governments throughout the region. The United States would look on approvingly and Cuban influence would recede.

Needless to say, the future of the Caribbean will most likely not follow either of these scenarios. The future is always full of surprises, some pleasant, others not. But whatever lies ahead for the Caribbean will depend largely on the people and governments of the area, the state of the Cuban-Soviet axis, and the policies of outside powers, chiefly the United States.

It is sometimes forgotten that most Caribbean countries have not been independent very long. Those that gained independence during the 19th century, Haiti and the Dominican Republic, lived through many agonizing years of poverty and oppression. In Haiti these conditions still exist. The rest of the Caribbean countries did not come into being as independent states until the past three decades. Some are but a few years old.

These young countries are still finding their way. Their leaders know that they must build societies that are strong, stable, and just. But how? The kind of economic growth that can make meaningful changes in the lives of their people will be difficult to achieve, and then only with strong help from the outside. Caribbean leaders are faced with difficult choices. Do they try to pattern their societies after Castro's Cuba, reducing the gap between rich and poor at the expense of real economic growth and personal liberty? Or do they try to emulate Puerto Rico, not in its association with the United States, but in its program of sharply raising the per capita income of the country through private-sector industrialization? Or do they produce local combinations of both models?

Cuba has been an unsettling force in the Caribbean since Castro seized power in Havana. But even the most determined revolutionaries have been known to mellow and adjust to realities. No one expects a dedicated Marxist-Leninist like Fidel Castro to change overnight and convert Cuba into a pro-Western democracy. But he has shown a willingness to negotiate with the United States without preconditions; earlier, he would not talk unless the American trade embargo against Cuba were lifted. During the administrations of presidents Gerald Ford and Jimmy Carter, talks were under way with Cuba on the subjects of maritime and fishing rights, air piracy, tourism, and cultural and academic exchanges. The talks were called off because of Cuba's military activities in Africa. But Cuba will not be in Africa forever. The time will come for a reopening of talks and possibly the renewal of U.S.–Cuban diplomatic ties.

In the case of a highly magnetic personality like Castro, the question inevitably arises: What happens to Cuba after Fidel? Similar questions were asked about other Communist leaders: "What will happen in the Soviet Union after Stalin?" "What will happen in China after Mao Zedong?" In both cases, the Marxist-Leninist structure and character of the state remained intact. But changes in leadership did bring many changes in policy, most noticeably in China but also in the Soviet Union. The same pattern probably will apply to Cuba.

The American role in the Caribbean certainly will not diminish in the decades ahead. The traditional U.S. economic, political, and strategic interests will remain. And, on a personal level, ties between America and the 30 million people of the Caribbean almost certainly will be strengthened as millions more people of the region and their descendants call the United States home.

What is the future of U.S. policy in the Caribbean? To some extent, this depends on the particular administration in Washington. Still, it is not hard to predict that containment of Castro's Cuba and Soviet influence will be a major element in U.S. policy for some time to come. Cuba will be watched carefully; but statesmanship may require that America at some point reach out the hand of civility, if not friendship, to Cuba's Communist dictatorship.

America's attitude toward the democracies of the Caribbean will be of extreme importance in the latter part of the 20th century. In the past, the United States has alternated between long periods of indifference toward the region and short periods of acute concern. Concern has manifested itself only when American interests have been believed to be threatened. In recent decades, U.S. administrations have reacted to the threat of Cuban and Soviet ambitions in the region, but only on occasion have they come forth with positive programs designed to bring progress to the area and strengthen its democracies. The question for the future is: Will the United States adopt a policy of sustained attention to the problems of the Caribbean, an area vital to its interests, or will it continue to alternate between indifference and something akin to panic?

Perhaps there is no easy answer to such a fundamental question. But the people of the Caribbean look to the United States for creative leadership and benevolent attention. It is a challenge, of course. But it is also a great opportunity.

FOR FURTHER READING

Students who wish to explore further the history, culture, and contemporary events of the Caribbean will find a rich variety of written material in libraries, in bookstores, and at newstands.

A useful, two-volume general history is *The Caribbean Story* by William Claypole and John Robottom (London and New York: Longman Group Ltd., 1981). The book covers Caribbean history from the original Indian settlers to the recent past; it is extremely well illustrated. Another interesting general history is *From Columbus to Castro: the History of the Caribbean* by Eric Williams (London: André Deutsch Ltd., 1970). Formerly prime minister of Trinidad and Tobago, an historian as well as a political leader, the late Dr. Williams addresses the history of the region with clarity and conviction.

A good book dealing with a specific period in Caribbean history is *The Spanish Caribbean: Trade and Plunder* by Kenneth R. Andrews (New Haven: Yale University Press, 1978). This work includes much colorful detail on the activities of traders and buccaneers during the Spanish heyday in the Caribbean.

A far different kind of history of the Caribbean is *A Family of Islands* by Alec Waugh (Garden City, New York: Doubleday & Co., Inc., 1964). Written by a novelist who knows the area intimately, the book is a perceptive, entertaining account of the Caribbean people from Columbus to the dawn of the 20th century. Another book by a contemporary literary figure is *The Middle Passage* by V. S. Naipaul (New York: Vintage Books, 1981). A Trinidadian of Indian ancestry, Naipaul returned to the Caribbean after years in England and wrote incisive portraits of five countries—Trinidad, British Guiana (Guyana), Suriname, Martinique, and Jamaica.

Thoughtful, clear, and compact is *The Caribbean: Its Implications for the United States* by Virginia R. Dominguez and Jorge I. Dominguez (New York: Headline Series—Foreign Policy Association, 1981). The authors, both Caribbean scholars, examine America's past role in the Caribbean and offer suggestions for future policy.

United States policy toward the Caribbean for the past 200 years is the subject of *U.S. Policy in the Caribbean* by John Bartlow Martin (New York: Twentieth Century Fund, 1978). Clearly written and well argued, the book is by a longtime journalist and a former U.S. ambassador to the Dominican Republic.

Students are also advised to consult the appropriate entries—"Caribbean," "Cuba," "Jamaica," etc.—in reference works such as the *Encyclopaedia Britannica*. Current affairs can be followed in newspapers with solid foreign coverage or in newsmagazines such as *Time* and *Newsweek*. An excellent source, available in many libraries, is the *Caribbean Review*.

INDEX

Japan, 85
Johnson, Lyndon B., 73–75
Jones Act, 1917, 34, 53

Kennedy, John Fitzgerald, 62–63, 70, 73
Khrushchev, Nikita, 63–64

Labor unions, 39–43
Leninism. *See* Marxism.
L'Ouverture, Touissaint, 20, 33

Machado, Gerardo, 55–56
McKinley, William, 28, 30
Magoon, Charles, 33
Maine (ship), 28
Manley, Michael, 66, 75
Manley, Norman, 44–45, 75
Manuel de Cespedes, Carlos, 56
Marshall Plan, 69
Marti, Jose, 28
Martinique, 8, 17, 48, 49
Marxism, 3, 4, 7, 56, 58, 66, 68, 77–78, 93, 95
Mexico, 7, 16, 82, 85, 93
Monroe Doctrine, 24–25, 31–32
   Roosevelt Corollary, 31–32, 35, 69, 74
Monroe, James, 24–25
Montserrat, 7
Moyne Commission report, 1944, 41–42
Muñoz Marin, Luis, 50–53

Naipaul, V.S., 5
Napoleon, 20
Netherlands, 16, 17, 18, 19, 21, 36, 46–48, 80–81
New Deal, 50
New Jewel Movement, 77
Nicaragua, 33, 35, 66, 74
Nina (ship), 10
North Korea, 77, 79

Operation Bootstrap, 50–52
Organization of American States, 63, 64, 73, 74, 82
Organization of Eastern Caribbean States, 78
Orinoco River, 11

Panama Canal, 31, 33, 34, 35, 85
Paraguay, 74
Peoples' Republic of China, 95
Peru, 16
Philippines, 28–29
Pierce, Franklin, 25
Pinero, Jesus T., 53
Pinta (ship), 10
Plantocracy, 18–21
Platt Amendment, 30, 56
Portugal, 18, 19, 66
Prio Socarras, Carlos, 57
Prussia, 24
Puerto Rico, 3, 7–8, 16, 21, 26, 27, 29–30, 34, 35, 37, 49–54, 88, 90–91, 94